THE WHALING YEARS

PETERHEAD
(1788 – 1893)

Centre for Scottish Studies, University of Aberdeen
Director and Editor of booklets: Dr John S. Smith (Department of Geography)
Editor of *Northern Scotland*: Professor Peter L. Payne (Department of History)
Conference Organiser: Mr A. Rodney Gunson (Department of Geography)
Northern Scotland is the annual journal of the Centre. Full details on subscription,
content and availability of back numbers on request.

Books in print pertinent to North East Scotland published by the Centre for Scottish
Studies, and available from the Centre.

D.P. Willis *Sand and Silence. Lost Villages of the North*	£3.00
David Toulmin *The Tillycorthie Story*	£4.50
Hazel Carnegie *Harnessing the Wind. Captain Thomas Mitchell of the White Star Line.*	£2.95
David Summers *Fishing off the Knuckle. The Story of Buchan's Fishing Villages*	£3.00
Nancy H. Miller *Peterhead and the Edinburgh Merchant Maidens. Visits by the Governors to their Buchan Estates, 1728–1987*	£3.00
Sinclair Ross *The Culbin Sands – Fact and Fiction*	£7.95
James S. Wood *For Heaven's Sake*	£3.00
Flora Youngson *Dominie's Daughter*	£3.50

Books in print pertinent to North East Scotland published by the Mercat Press
sponsored by and available from the Centre.

Fermfolk and Fisherfolk – Rural Life in Northern Scotland, edited by John S. Smith and David Stevenson	£6.95
Grampian Battlefields – the Historic Battles of North East Scotland, Peter Marren.	£9.95
Shipwrecks of North East Scotland 1444–1990, David M. Ferguson.	£6.95
Rural Life in Victorian Aberdeenshire, William Alexander.	£6.95
North East Castles. Castles in the Landscape of N.E. Scotland edited by John S. Smith.	£5.95
Old Aberdeen: Bishops, Burghers and Buildings, edited by John S. Smith	£5.95
The Diary of a Canny Man 1818–1828. Adam Mackie, Farmer, Innkeeper and Merchant in Fyvie, edited by David Stevenson	£6.95

Centre for Scottish Studies
University of Aberdeen
The Old Brewery, High Street
Old Aberdeen AB9 2UB
Tel. 0224 272474

THE WHALING YEARS

PETERHEAD
(1788 – 1893)

Gavin Sutherland

Illustrated by Dianne Sutherland

Centre for Scottish Studies
University of Aberdeen

First published 1993
© Centre for Scottish Studies, University of Aberdeen 1993

British Library Cataloguing in Publication Data

A catalogue record for this book is available from the British Library.

ISBN 0 906265 17 7

Typeset: Hewer Text Composition Services, Edinburgh
Printed: BPCC–AUP Ltd, Aberdeen

This book is dedicated to
Kelly, Emily and Lorna

I would like to thank 'Peter' F G Wernham
for his kind and willing assistance.

To play a salmon is a royal game, but when your fish weighs more than a suburban villa, and is worth a clear two thousand pounds, it dwarfs all other experiences.

Dr Arthur Conan Doyle, 'The Idler', 1892

Bowhead or Greenland Right, hunted almost to extinction by nineteenth century whalers.

If whales are as intellectually advanced as the scientific community believes, their slaughter is as abominable and as immoral as killing humans.

Dr David Weeks, *Press & Journal*, 1992

CONTENTS

List of Illustrations   vii
Acknowledgements   xi
John Rennie 1836-1917   xiii
Captain David Gray III   xv

The Early Days   1
Hunting the Davis Straits   5
Recovery of the Active   14
The Greenland Sea Boys   16
The Price of Success   23
The Prince's First Command   29
The Maiden Voyage of the *Active*   32
The Summit of Peterhead's Ambition   37
Iron and Ice   52
SS *Eclipse* – 'The Black Prince'   70
David Gray, the Naturalist   91
Hope For Sale   103
The End of an Era   108

The Grays of Peterhead   113
Bibliography   123

ILLUSTRATIONS

Bowhead or Greenland Right, hunted almost to extinction
  by nineteenth century whalers.   vi
Peterhead Harbours, 1869 (OS map)   x
John Rennie   xiii
Captain David Gray III   xv
Striking a Bowhead.   3
Extract from the 1796 Muster Roll of the 64 gun Man-of-War,
  Ardent.   7
Surgeon below decks at Camperdown   9
Peterhead Bay 1813, by George Tytler   10
The Fleet of 1814   11

Captain William Scoresby's 'Comparative View'. *An Account of the Arctic Regions* 12
Inuit (Eskimo), of Greenland, Sir John Ross 17
John Gray's Master's Ticket 19
'Baffin Fair', 1830 (artist unknown) 20
Captain John Gray I 22
The Foy 24
Quayside farewell 25
Scrimshaw. 28
Whaler beset 30
James Hogg's headstone 31
Log of the *Eclipse*, June 1852 34
Ptarmigans and white hare 36
Active in the South Harbour, 1853 38
Saddleback and pup 40
Neptune and the Greenhand 42
Tools of the trade 44
Winching baleen on deck 46
All hands making off blubber 47
Style - at any price 48
An encounter with polar bears 50
List of Sailings from Bressay Sound 54
Northern Fisheries report 55
The *Traveller* and the old *Eclipse* were both wrecked in 1858 56, 57
The value of a whaler 58
The Shipwrecked Mariners' Society - compensation for loss at sea 60
Buchan fishwives travelled throughout the districts trading fish for farm goods 61
Harpoon head 62
Richmond House 63
Letter from the RNLI to Captain David Gray 67
A temporary reprieve for a walrus herd as the Hammerfest hunters pass to the north 68
Clifton House, Peterhead, 1880 69
SS *Eclipse* in the Greenland ice 71
Scale model of SS *Eclipse* made by Captain Gray's youngest son, James 72
Model of a whale boat of the Peterhead type from that same era 73
Robert Walker Gray on board SS *Eclipse* with his father, 1888 76
Crow's Nest 77

David Gray's famous sailing ship *Active* was fitted for steam
    in 1871 while under the command of Captain 'Oily Bob'
    Martin.   79
Active for sale   80
Shipping blubber, and Narwhal on deck   81
'The Great Northern Diver'   83
The crew of SS *Hope* outside the boilyards, Keith Inch, *c*.1880   84
The 'Seahorse' and the 'Unicorn'   85
Making off walrus skins   86
Bottlenose whale   87
Notes and harpooners' table from the log of the *Eclipse*, 1882   88
SS *Mazinthien*, aground in Peterhead Bay, 17 March 1883   89
Lost in a Greenland fog   90
Seal pup   92
'Linnets' and Albatross   94
Fulmar, Glaucous Gull and Little Auks   96
Peterhead Broadgate, *c*.1890   98
'The Rescuers'. Expedition leader Sir Allen William Young
    with the crew of the *Hope*, 1882   99
SS *Hope* leaving the North Harbour, by William Hutton   100
Whale alongside the *Eclipse*   101
Hope for sale in 1887 – set of plans and information drawn up
    for the French Canadian market   102
'The Links', Peterhead (1880-1991)   105
Antarctic scene   107
SS *Windward* – last of the Peterhead whalers – in the North
    Harbour   108
A home on the frozen deep   111
David Gray and Bob, 1888   112
The family of Captain David Gray III and Amelia
    Walker, 1888   115

Front cover:

The whaler SS *Eclipse*, by William Birnie of Peterhead, *c*.1870,
    courtesy of Mr V Bruce, great grandson of Captain David Gray III.
Back cover:
Illustrated Map by Dianne Sutherland.

Peterhead Harbours, 1869 (extract from OS map)

ACKNOWLEDGEMENTS

Thanks are due to North East Scotland Museums Service; to the Aberdeen City, North East Scotland, British, Guildhall and Queen Mother Libraries; Dr John Smith and Dr Robert Ralph (Aberdeen University); Dr David Bertie, Alex Buchan, Stephen Caine, Jill Dick, James George Eddison, Paul E. Hartley, Norman Hurst, James D. Johnston, Marjorie Leith, George Sutherland, Iain Sutherland, Barry Wain, Peter and Mrs F. Wernham, and Duncan Wood. Special thanks to Nina Jenkins (London) and Diane Baptie (Edinburgh) for their diligent research work, and to Rex Findlay (photographer Arbuthnot Museum, Peterhead), Gordon Junner (Aberdeen Family History Society), Mormon Church Library, Aberdeen, Janice Murray (Dundee Museum), Ian Gentle (Royal Museum of Scotland), Mhairi McCrane, Neil Murray; The Peterhead Harbour Board, and all at ACS, Banff and 'Network 90', Macduff.

Thank you all for your help and encouragement.

ILLUSTRATIONS

Dianne Sutherland: The Bowhead (vi); Striking a Bowhead (3); Surgeon below decks at Camperdown (9); The Foy (24); A Quayside Farewell (25); Scrimshaw (28); Whaler beset (30); Ptarmigan and white hare (36); *Active* in the South Harbour (38); Saddleback and pup (40); Neptune and the Greenhand (42); Tools of the Trade (44); Style-at any price (48); An encounter with bears (50); Buchan fishwives at the station (61); Harpoon head (62); Richmond House (63); 'A Temporary Reprieve' (68); Clifton House (69); Crow's Nest (77); 'The Great Northern Diver' (83); The 'seahorse' and the 'unicorn' (85); Linnets and Albatross (94); The Fulmar, Glaucous Gull and Little Auks (96).

Other:
Peterhead Bay, 1813, George Tytler, courtesy of Arbuthnot Museum (10); Inuit Family, Sir John Ross, 1824 (17); Baffin Fair (artist unknown), 1830 (20); Captain John Gray, courtesy of F G Wernham

(22); *Hope* Leaving Harbour, William Hutton, courtesy of Arbuthnot Museum. (100).

PHOTOGRAPHS:

Arbuthnot Museum: *Eclipse* in the Greenland Ice (71); Captain David Gray and Robert Walker Gray (76); Crew of the *Hope* 1880 (84); *Mazinthien* aground at Peterhead (89); Crew of the *Hope* 1882 (99); *Windward* in Peterhead (108); David Gray and 'Bob' (111).
Dundee Museums: Hauling whalebone aboard (46); All hands making off blubber (47); *Active* in the Greenland ice (79); Shipping blubber and Narwhal on deck (81); Making off walrus skins (86); Bowhead alongside *Eclipse* (101).
Natural History Museum, London: A home on the frozen deep (111)
Royal Museums, Edinburgh: Model of *Eclipse* (72); Model of whaleboat (73).
University of Aberdeen, George Washington Wilson Collection: Peterhead Broadgate (98).

Other:
Sheila Moffat: The Links, Peterhead
F G Wernham: The Gray Family,
Author's collection: John Rennie

The photographs on pp. 71, 76, 111 and 112 are from a series taken by W Livingstone Learmouth, Captain's guest aboard SS *Eclipse*, Greenland Sea, 1888.

JOHN RENNIE
(the author's great, great, grandfather)
1836–1917

John Rennie was a cooper's son from Rosehearty, whose family, like many others in the 1840s, bundled together what little they had and headed for Peterhead, the north east's thriving 'Blubberopolis'.

John began his long career with the Greenland whaling fleet as a thirteen year old apprentice cooper, working six months at sea and six months ashore making barrels for the herring trade.

By 1857 Peterhead had grown to become Europe's principal whaling station. A fleet of thirty-one ships left for the Arctic that year, crewed by more than a thousand men. The industry had brought great changes; seven thousand people now lived in the town, more than doubling the population in less than sixty years. It would have been hard to convince even the most sceptical of those involved that the 'palmy days' would soon be over, and by the turn of the century nothing but memories of the industry would remain.

During research into my own family's history I became fascinated by my home town's whaling enterprise and the community who shared its successes and failures.

The following pages tell the remarkable tale as witnessed by the Grays of Peterhead, a whaling family who, for three generations, stood at the forefront of the town's original oil boom.

Gavin Sutherland, 1993

In no industry did physical nature so predominate as in the whale and seal fishing. This is what made it at once dangerous and uncertain; in it fortunes were suddenly acquired and as suddenly squandered. A well-known civic dignitary of Peterhead used to say: 'If you have any money and don't know what to do with it, buy a Greenland ship; if you have any more left, buy another!'

Captain Alexander Geary commanded the first Peterhead whaler; his grandson, Captain David Gray, the last. This old family represented all that was best in the history of the Peterhead whale fishery. Their success in it is beyond comparison. The grandfathers and father of Captain David Gray were great and successful whalers, but he eclipsed them all; he was 'The Prince of Whalers'.

J T Findlay's 'History of Peterhead'
Buchan Observer, 1896

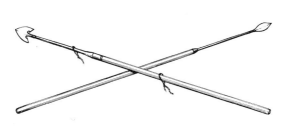

CAPTAIN DAVID GRAY III, 1828–1896
Peterhead, Aberdeenshire

David Gray was born in October 1828, the son of Captain John Gray and Barbara Geary. His home in Castle Street, Keith Inch, was at the heart of a close-knit island community that owed its existence to the sea, and had for generations produced mariners and fishermen whose skills and accomplishments were second to none.

David and his younger brothers, John and Alexander, absorbed the influences of their neighbourhood's industry from their earliest years, and encouraged by their father, as he had been by his father a generation before, grew up to follow the family's maritime traditions. Young David's respect for the sea was profound. When only five years old he witnessed the tragic death of his grandfather, and narrowly escaped death himself, when their small fishing boat capsized in Peterhead Bay. While his grandfather swam for help David somehow clung to the hull of the upturned boat until help arrived. His grandfather's body was washed ashore the following morning.

Ten years later David went to the whaling for the first time as an apprentice in his father's ship, the *Eclipse*. He rose through the ranks quickly and took his first command, as Captain of the whale ship *North of Scotland*, when barely out of his 'teens. His association with the '*North*' earned David Gray the privileged respect of ships' officers and crewmen alike, and it was not long before he joined the ranks of Peterhead's seafaring elite, a handful of men whose spirited labour and bold adventure had restored the struggling north-east fishing town's pride and sense of importance.

From the first he displayed all the gifts and qualifications of a successful navigator and whaler.

Captain Gray was a seaman of the best type; but he was more than a seaman. His interest in the animal life of the Arctic regions was the interest of a naturalist, and the information which he supplied to the Royal Society and some of the Geographical Societies was looked upon as invaluable. For his knowledge of the natural laws of the country he had no compeer.

With a staid and characteristic dignity of his own, he impressed strangers at once as a man of distinction. His own success was genuine, and in every department of life he attributed success to a man's making himself thoroughly and intelligently master of his own work.

Peterhead Sentinel & Buchan Journal, Tuesday 19 May 1896

The Early Days

The Peterhead Greenland Fishing commenced in 1788, and for four-teen years the *Robert* of 169 tons with a crew of thirty-six was the only vessel employed. The first ten years [two under Captain Harrison and eight under William Peacock, of Hull] were very unsuccessful, owing, it is supposed, to the master and greater part of the crew who were Englishmen, being bribed not to exert themselves, in case Peterhead should enter farther into the fisheries which they had all along attempted to monopolise. They were, therefore on the point of giving it entirely up, when two gentlemen, Mr James Arbuthnot and Mr John Hutchison, suggested the propriety of manning the vessel with seamen and fishermen of this place, which was done, and Mr Geary, a native of Peterhead, received a command.

The Peterhead Kalendar, 1853

Alexander Geary, a sailor's son from Peterhead's Ronheads, had served on the *Robert* as a mate since her earliest days at Peterhead, and in the words of a shipmate was 'the best harpooner in her, and a capital sailor!' His promotion to commander, in 1798, brought a sudden change of fortune to the old ship; four whales were captured on her first trip under Geary, delivering more than seventy tons of precious oil.

At 169 tons—a size no doubt dictated by the state of Peterhead harbour, which at the time was little more than a tidal creek—the *Robert* was barely fit for Arctic work, but, nevertheless, continued to struggle through a further four productive seasons before being sold and replaced by the *Hope*, again under Geary, in 1803.

The *Hope*, at 240 tons, was a superior vessel, and far better equipped for the polar seas. On her first voyage out of Peterhead the new ship took eleven whales and brought home more than 117 tons of blubber, proof that with the right ship the local sailors could hold their own with the long established southern fleets.

At about this time Geary and his associates formed Peterhead's first whaling company, setting up headquarters on Keith Inch. They bought the granary at the south of the island, by old Keith Castle, and converted the malt barn and kiln into a boil-house and stores. With business booming the whaler *Enterprise* joined the *Hope* in 1804, Geary's first mate, William Volum, her new commander.

1

WHALES IN PETERHEAD BAY

In 1806, a year best remembered for the opening of the new parish church, 'The Muckle Kirk', Geary and Volum were involved in a whale hunt much closer to home. In mid October a Greenland Right Whale and her calf came into Peterhead Bay and as word spread through the town people rushed down to the shore to watch the hunt. For the young lads who had heard so much of Greenland from fathers and grandfathers who had been there many times, it was a very special day, a day they would not forget.

Two of those lads were old men when, in 1880, they told their story to Geary's grandson, Captain David Gray III. Gray was investigating the event on behalf of Thomas Southwell, a naturalist who shared his interest in Arctic mammals, and was keen to learn the facts of the matter.

T. Southwell Esq, Norwich.   3rd Dec. 1880.
                                                                     Peterhead.
My Dear Sir,
The facts of the case you will find in the enclosed depositions of John Allen and James Webster, both eye witnesses. I also find from other witnesses that Capt. William Volum of the *Enterprise* and Capt. Alex. Geary of the *Hope* both took part in the chase. I may mention that both Allen and Webster spent the whole of their lives as Harpooners in the Greenland Whalefishing.
James Webster, 85 years of age, remembers the Greenland Whales coming into South Bay of Peterhead—at that time he would have been about 10 years of age. He remembers there being an old whale and a sucker [young calf]. He saw five boats go after them. They struck the old whale, put three harpoons in her, then they struck the sucker and killed it. The old whale stove two of the boats and broke harpooner Mackie's legs.
John Allen, 84 years of age, remembers the old whale, after being struck, going round the South Head. A heavy sea being on at the time and coming down dark, say about 10 or 11 o'clock, they followed her as far as they could before they cut two of the boats from her and left her towing one boat, with her Jack blowing, after taking her crew out of her, and in this condition the Whale went out of sight and they never saw or heard of her again. They killed the young whale and flenched her [cut the blubber from the carcass] at the South Quay—she having sunk it was two or three days after, before they got her in.
I have no doubt in my own mind that these whales were the true Greenland Whale.
                    I am dear Sir, Yours truely,
                            David Gray.

Striking a Bowhead.

With most of the English whalers, and the southern Scots, preferring to hunt at Davis Straits those few who frequented the Greenland Sea continued to do well. With good numbers of whales and seals in the waters off Greenland and Spitzbergen the *Hope* and *Enterprise* returned to port more often than not 'full ship'.

> Yesterday arrived at Peterhead from the Greenland Whale Fishery the *Hope*, Geary, and the *Enterprise*, Volum, the former with 26 and the latter with 21 fish—full ships.
> *Aberdeen Chronicle*, Saturday 22 July 1809

Geary's bumper catch of 1809 marked his last voyage north. Old 'Sandy the Pioneer' was in poor health on his return from Greenland. He died four months later.

Captain George Sangster became master of the *Hope* in 1810, and another Peterheadian, Captain John Souter, joined the hunt with the ship *Active* that same year. Souter had for some time been engaged in the transportation of emigrant Scots to the 'Americas', and during those often troublesome voyages he had proved his worth as a sailor many times. In 1808, for instance, as the *Active* made her way home from Newfoundland, she ran into a dreadful mid-Atlantic gale. Souter met with the Londoner, *Reliance*, badly damaged and in dire straits, and, notwithstanding the awful conditions, he put his ship alongside the crippled *Reliance* and took the desperate crew aboard. Two of the ship-wrecked men died before the *Active* made Ullapool on 21 February—they had been at sea for more than three months!

Even after his first gruelling season at the Greenland whaling Souter took his ship to the west coast for an Atlantic crossing. He planned to deliver his party of emigrants to Nova Scotia and then make north for the whaling grounds at Davis Straits. The *Active* left Oban in early October, but after only a few days bad weather forced her to turn tail and run for home. The ill-fated voyage was to be the last the *Active* made as a passenger vessel and marked the beginning of a new career for both ship and master.

Captain David Gray I

'We have the pleasure of stating that the Peterhead whaling ships are all arrived full, particulars as follows:

Active, Souter, 26 fish, 180 tons: *Hope*, Sangster, 27 fish, 150 tons; *Enterprise*, Volum, 31 fish, 165 tons; and *Perseverance*, Gray, 25 fish, 150 tons.'

Aberdeen Chronicle—Ship News,
Saturday 3 August 1811

The owners of Peterhead's latest ship, *Perseverance*, commissioned Captain David Gray of South Shields for the season of 1811. In December 1810, shortly after his family's arrival in Peterhead, the Captain's wife gave birth to a third son, George Arbuthnot Gray. Named after his father's new employer he was the first of the Grays to be born in Peterhead for two generations at least.

MUTINEERS AND HEROES

The earliest records of the captain's career show that he joined King George III's Navy in 1796. He was twenty-two years old when he volunteered and on receipt of his £5 bounty Able Seaman Gray was assigned to *Ardent*, a sixty-four gun ship of the line.

He had been with the ship only a year when she joined a mutinous North Sea fleet at the Great Nore, off Sheerness, in militant protest against poor pay, dreadful conditions, and the brutalities of naval discipline.

On 5 June 1797 the rebel fleet formed a blockade at the mouth of the Thames and took control over the passage of ships to and from London. Officers were held hostage; some were flogged, others tarred and feathered and rowed through the fleet before being dumped on the shore at Gravesend. While delegates from the 'Floating Republic' negotiated with the Admiralty, conditions on board the ships grew steadily worse. Men took the law into their own often drunken hands and those judged to be 'failing to support the mutiny wholeheartedly' were punished severely, either by 'ducking'—weighted and plunged into the sea until almost drowned—or, like four of the *Ardent*'s men found guilty of 'disrespect', 'put to the mast' and lashed.

When a company of West Yorks Militia were posted along the coast to prevent the rebels coming ashore for food and fresh water the mutiny began to crumble. Divided loyalties led to chaos and one by one, often under fire from those determined to hold out, ships broke from the pack and ran for Gravesend in surrender. The last ship to take down its defiant Red Flag was the mutineers' 'flagship', the *Sandwich*. She gave up on 13 June and Richard Parker, 'President' of the mutinous republic, was duly arrested, court martialled, and hanged.

Though many rebels faced the courts only twenty-nine were executed. The Dutch were about to challenge the Royal Navy's supremacy in the German Ocean and 'Old Farmer George'—still reeling from the loss of his American colonies—needed all the help he could get.

THE BATTLE OF CAMPERDOWN

On 11 October 1797 Admiral Duncan's reformed North Sea Fleet faced the Dutch off Camperdown, where once more Able Seaman David Gray had found himself a 'very hot berth'. The *Ardent*, under Captain Richard Burgess, was one of eighteen British ships to face a Dutch fleet of twenty-three, and at 1 pm was the first to engage the enemy flagship, *Vrijheid*.

Within the first ten minutes Captain Burgess lay dead. Mr Dunn (ship's master) was killed moments later and two lieutenants badly wounded. In the following three hours of mayhem forty of the ship's company lay dead and ninety-six injured.

Lieutenant Philip, in charge after his Captain's death, reported:

> I am afraid that a great part of our wounded will die, as they are in general dreadfully mangled. One of the men's wives assisted in firing a gun where her husband was quartered, though frequently requested to go below, but she would not be prevailed on to do so until a shot carried away one of her legs and wounded the other. As to the damage done to the ship, a description of it would fill sheets of paper. It is indeed a wonder from the number of shot holes in her sides that we had not many more men killed. The first two broadsides of the Dutch were terrible; but after that, on average, the British fired three guns to their one.

Bounty Paid	N°	Entry.	Year	Appear-ance.	Whence and whether Prest or not.	Place and County where Born.	Age at Time of Entry in this Ship.	N° and Letter of Tickets.	MENS NAMES.	Qualities.	D. D.D. or R.	Time of Discharge.
£7.10.0	121	20 Aug	1796	Sept 29	SL & Vol OE & Ch3 N° 117 Vol	Warwich Geo	20		Jn° Reid	AB		
5.0.0	"	"	"	"	do 118 Vol	America	30		Benj° Weeks	ab		
	"	"	"	"	119 Ot	C° of Guinea	10		Chas Reading	Lm		
	21	"	"	"	120 Ot				Jn° Williams(6)	ab	L/q	11 Oct°
5.0.0	5	"	"	"	121 Vol	S° Shields	22		Dav° Gray	ab		
5.0.0	"	"	"	"	122 Vol	Berwick on Tweed	23		Jn° Brown(4)	AB	R	23 Dec°
2.10.0	"	"	"	"	123 Vol	N° Shields	22		Wm Turner(2)	Ad°		
	14	"	"	"	124 Ot	Yarmouth Norfolk	35		Isaac Jones	ab		
	"	"	"	"	125 Ot	Cambleton Scotd	21		Alex° Watson	Ord°		
4.10.0	30	30	"	"	"	SLwith OE N°	London	20		Thos Charters	Lm		
4.10.0		"	"	"	"		London	20		Wm Boyd	Lm		
2.10.0		3 Sept	"	"	"	N3V 165	Carmarthen S° Wales	21		Wm Jones 5 October 1796 - Cap	Ord° Seaman	R	20 Feby
2.10.0		"	"	"	"	166	Witby York	20		Rich° Wrangham	Ord°		
2.10.0		"	"	"	"	167	Honiton Devon	20		Jn° Campbell	Ord°		
	6	"	"	"	"	168 Ot Salm°	32		Jas Johns	ab	L/q	31 Jan°
		"	"	"	"	N3V 150	Nevis	20		Chas Willard	Ord°		
		"	"	"	"	151 Ot	Maryland	31		Jacob Deacon	Ord°		
		"	"	"	"	153 Ot	New York America	28		Jn° Sanson, Cornhill	Ord°		
	29	"	"	"	Substitute	Pilkington Lincoln	25		Wm Thompson	Ord°		
No 6. 140	140	6 Sept	"	Oct 1	Standard seckers	Froome Somerset	22		Jn° Brown Juskis	Lm		

Extract from the 1796 Muster Roll of the 64 gun Man-of-War, *Ardent*, recording the arrival of Volunteer 121, Able Seaman David Gray of South Shields. *Crown copyright, by permission of HMSO ADM 36/12392.*

'VICTORY'

Hats and bonnets were tossed in the air as the cheering Yarmouth crowds welcomed home Duncan's victorious fleet. The *Ardent*, her masts and steering gear destroyed by the enemy's merciless cannonade, limped into port with the help of a cable from the *Bedford* —the ship that had stood at her side throughout the fearful ordeal.

Some of the worst horrors were witnessed by ship's surgeon Robert Young, who for more than twelve hours had fought to do what he could for the wounded piled around him.

> So great was my fatigue, [Young later wrote], that I began several amputations under a dread of sinking before I had secured the blood vessels.
>
> About 16 mortally wounded died after they were brought down, amongst whom was the brave and worthy Capt. Burgess. Joseph Bonheur had his right thigh taken off by a cannon shot close to the pelvis, so that it was impossible to apply a tourniquet; his right arm was also shot to pieces. All the service I could render this unfortunate man was to put dressings over the part and give him drink.
>
> Melancholy cries for assistance were addressed to me from every side by wounded and dying, and piteous moans and bewailing from pain and despair. The man whose leg I first amputated had not uttered a groan from the time he was brought down, and several, exulting in the news of the victory, declared they regretted not the loss of their limbs.

After suffering the hardship of the Nore Mutiny and the carnage of Camperdown Able Seaman Gray had, understandably, had enough, and when the *Ardent* put into Chatham three months later for repairs he abandoned ship and fled for the north of England. Desertion was commonplace, and although records of 'run men' were kept, little effort was made to track down the culprits, who could be more easily replaced by press gangs.

After a time 'on the run' Gray married Lily Cowan (*c*.1800), a Scottish lowland lass, and for a while settled in South Shields. It was there that he took a berth on a whaler, and so began a famous career.

---

facing page

Surgeon below decks at Camperdown. 'Melancholy cries for assistance were addressed to me from every side . . .'

Peterhead Bay 1813, by George Tytler.

'FORTY AND FOUR WHALES'

Peterhead had a fleet of seven ships by 1814, the foundation of an industry that was destined to thrive beyond all expectation. Britain was in the throes of the Industrial Revolution, and with the potential of mineral oil as yet untapped, the demand for whale blubber to light the lamps and grease the wheels of progress had never been greater.

Political unrest in Europe had all but destroyed foreign competition and Peterhead, with shrewd financial support, and a pool of experienced navigators and expert boatmen, was fast becoming one of Europe's principal whaling stations.

> There are not finer built vessels in Britain than those of Peterhead, and it is in a great measure owing to this, that they have been so successful at the Greenland Whale Fishery, as they can venture among the ice when other vessels of a more slender build are obliged to keep aloof.
>
> 'An Historical Account of Peterhead', 1815
> J. Arbuthnot

WHALE AND SEAL FISHING.

1814 is ever to be remembered in the annals of the Peterhead whale fishing. The following are the statistics of that most successful year:—

1814.						Tuns
Tonnage.	Ships.	Captains.	Seals.	Whales.		Oil.
1. 240	Hope ...	T. Philips	—	14		157
2. 290	Enterprise ...	A. Geary	—	24		183
3. 308	Active ...	D. Gray	—	22		232
4. 240	Perseverance	W. Penny	—	17		151
5. 400	Resolution ...	J. Suttar	—	44		299
6. 225	Union ...	W. Hutchison	—	17		172
7. 321	Dexterity ...	G. Sangster	—	25		196
				163		1390

Average, 198¼ tuns oil.

The Fleet of 1814.

John Souter of the *Resolution* made the record books in 1814 when he captured forty-four whales – many of them calves or 'suckers'. The hunt was a grim and merciless affair and few of its perpetrators concerned themselves with the consequences – money was there for the making and Peterhead's needs were great.

Rathen born shipmaster William Penny (*Perseverance*) was the father of one of Peterhead's best known navigators. Born in 1808, William Penny Jnr served with the local fleet before becoming master of the Aberdeen whaler *Neptune*. He made his mark in maritime history in 1850 as the leader of the *Lady Franklin* and *Sophia* expedition to the Canadian arctic in an attempt to unravel the mystery of Sir John Franklin's disappearance during his search for the North West Passage.

At the age of 21, Alex Geary Jnr was in his second year of command. Two years later he replaced George Sangster (his uncle) as master of the *Dexterity*. The ship's owner, William Volum (late of the *Enterprise*), had retired from the sea in 1811 to farm the nearby estate of Clerkhill and manage his shipping business. Geary Jnr died aboard the *Dexterity* as he brought his ship home from Greenland in 1819. He was 27 years old.

British Ports Engaged in the Whale-fishery.	Number of Ships.			Amount of Cargoes Obtained.			Average Cargo *per* Ship each Year.		
	Equipped in Four Years.	Average *per* Year.	Lost in Four Years.	Number of Whales.	Tons of Oil.	Tons of Whale-bone.	Number of Whales.	Tons of Oil.	Tons of Whale-bone.
London,	77	19¼	2	775	6,631	346	10.1	86.1	4.5
Hull,	229	57¼	3	1785	20,891	1064	7.8	91.2	4.6
Whitby,	39	9¾	0	433	4,181	201	11.1	107.2	5.2
Newcastle,	23	5¾	1	164	2,295	108	7.1	99.8	4.7
Other English Ports,	24	6	1	191	1,826	87	8.0	76.1	3.6
Total from England,	392	98	7	3348	35,824	1806	8.5	91.4	4.6
Aberdeen,	55	13¾	0	427	4,618	225	7.8	84.0	4.1
Leith,	40	10	0	278	3,756	170	7.0	93.9	4.2
Peterhead,	33	8¼	0	402	3,815	187	12.2	115.6	5.7
Dundee,	32	8	0	248	3,496	159	7.7	109.2	5.0
Montrose,	15	3¾	0	127	1,169	62	8.5	78.0	4.1
Other Ports in Scotland,	19	4¾	1	200	1,830	88	10.5	96.3	4.6
Total from Scotland,	194	48½	1	1682	18,684	891	8.7	96.3	4.6
Total from Britain.	586	146½	8	5030	54,508	2697	8.6	93.0	4.6

Captain William Scoresby's 'Comparative View 1814-1817'. *An Account of the Arctic Regions*, Vol II.

With harbour trade thriving , the 'Proprietors and Superiors' of Peterhead petitioned Parliament for a share of 'certain Balances arising from the forfeited [Jacobite] estates in Scotland towards making canals, harbours, and other public works'.

'With respect to the Greenland Fishery, which the Legislature has so warmly and wisely encouraged as of so much importance to the country in general, Peterhead possesses considerable advantage from its experienced Fishermen and from its being the first land made on their return by the ships in that Trade. Eight vessels belonging to and fitted out at Peterhead are this year employed in the Greenland Fishery.'

Taken from the Harbour Trustees' Petition to Parliament, signed by Roderick Gray on behalf of the Sederunt of 12 June 1816.

A WHALER'S BOUNTY

To encourage the development of the dangerous and hostile industry (and in so doing provide the navy with a free training ground) a Government Bounty was paid to ships of over 200 tons burthen. The following record shows the details of such a payment made to the whaler *Active* shortly before the scheme was withdrawn in the mid 1820s.

BOUNTY PAYMENT, 10 OCTOBER 1820.
THE WHALESHIP *ACTIVE*, 311 TONS BURTHEN. £300
CAPTAIN DAVID GRAY

Surgeon: William Adams, Mate: John Ogston.
Fished 19 March 1820—14 June 1820.
Stopped at Shetland 8 March for additional hands, and 24 June on homeward passage. Brought back produce of 4 whales and 4,500 seals.
Harpooners:
Alex Thomson, William Wiseman, Thomas Pringle, Thomas Davie, Charles Hay, George Irvine.
Boat Steersmen:
Alex Stewart, Wm. Abernethy, Wm. Mitchell, Wm. Fraser, John Freeman, Wm. Walker.
Line Managers:
George Simpson, James Walker, John Grieves, John Hay, Wm. Catto, Wm. Wilkinson.
Sailors:
Daniel Sheerbrook, John Reatie, Alex Reatie, George Ogstoune, Wm. Cowie, Bruce Robertson, Wm. Walker, Wm. MacPherson, Alex Emsley, John Potts, George Fife.
Apprentices:
Richard Davidson, James Duncan, Charles Sim, John Gray, George Seller, Alex Philip.
Green Men:
Andrew Smith, Abraham Alestone, George Willcox, Arthur Grieves, John Stephen, John Adams.

First Mate, John Ogston, and line managers George Simpson and James Walker, went on to become masters. The Captain's son, John Gray, is listed as the ship's fourth apprentice. He was fourteen years old and had just completed his second Arctic voyage. Young John was destined to become one of Peterhead's most famous sons, enjoying a long and colourful career as a Master Whaler.

Hunting the Davis Straits

The year 1821 marked a new phase in the history of Peterhead's fleet. Over-fishing the Greenland Sea resulted in a scarcity of whales there and some skippers began to chance their luck in the far off Davis Straits, sometimes using the Newfoundland port of St John's as a supply and recruiting station.

Seal hunting on the Labrador coast and whaling the Straits brought new problems to the Peterhead men. The inlets, bays and basins of the North American Arctic Archipelago were notoriously dangerous, and prone to sudden and drastic changes of weather. Ships could very quickly find themselves 'nipped' in the ice and could remain beset for days, weeks, or even months on end.

THE BROTHERHOOD OF LONERS AND MISFITS

> The ice was here, the ice was there,
> The ice was all around,
> It cracked and growled and roared and howled,
> Like noises in a swound.
>
> Anon

In a letter to the Aberdeen Herald, dated December 1842 and signed 'A Whaler', a sailor told of how his ship had been caught in the ice at Melville Sound during a whaling voyage in the mid 1820s. As the crew struggled to get stores and valuables off the stricken vessel and on to the ice, a party of men from a nearby American whaler, which was likewise beset, came to their assistance.

The 'Yanks', like the crew American novelist Herman Melville sent to hunt down the monstrous 'Moby Dick', were from every corner of the globe; the kind of misfits on whom his pagan harpooner characters Dagoo, the African, Tashtego, the Gay Head Indian, and Queequeg the tattooed Maori, had been based—a strange breed of men who were only at ease when in the company of fellow loners—Melville's 'isolatoes'.

The first task was to light fires around the ship and their makeshift camp on the ice; without fires the men would soon have frost-bite to add to their discomfort, as well as threats from wandering polar bears who could smell a blubber cargo from many miles away. When all that could be shifted was safely on the ice the men set about the business of making shelters—driving spars into the ice and draping them with sail cloth. With this done, and the immediate dangers over, an eight gallon barrel of brandy was struck open with a boat-axe, and huddled around the fires in the mellow Arctic light all hands proceeded to get 'glorious drunk!'

Several days later the ships got free. 'I could have leaped with joy as I saw the canvas again spread out to the breeze and heard the ripple of water alongside as the ship parted the tiny waves.'

The herrings regularly visit this part of the coast about the month of August; and now the lighthouse upon Buchanness will soon be completed it may be expected that Peterhead and Boddam will become stations for the herring fishing equal to any others on the east coast.
Aberdeen Chronicle, Saturday 3 September 1825
[From a report describing how vast shoals of herring were forced into Peterhead Bay by a school of Finner Whales.]

The Recovery of the *Active*

It was at Davis Straits that John Gray, then mate aboard his father's ship, *Active*, first made a name for himself.

> In 1825, the *Active* was enclosed in an inlet by a barrier of ice from which she could not be extricated. Mr John Gray was then sailing with his father. In the succeeding year, 1826, Captain David Gray proceeded to Davis Straits with the *Perseverance*, taking an extra crew with him for the purpose of looking for and bringing home the deserted ship. The *Active* was found where left, without having suffered any injury.
>
> Mr John Gray, then about 20 years of age, was placed on board the *Active* by his father, in the capacity of Master, and he brought her home, Captain David Gray remaining to prosecute the fishing with the *Perseverance*.
>
> *Aberdeen Free Press & Buchan News*
> Friday 19 September 1856

On Saturday 16 September 1826, the *Aberdeen Chronicle* reported the safe return of the *Active* and John Gray described how he and his father found the ship at Exeter Sound only a few hundred yards from where she had been left the previous year. The floe that had held her so firmly had all but disappeared and the ship lay beached in ten feet of water. A spirit bottle and a jug of ale, the remains of the crew's last toast to the ship before they abandoned her, stood where they had been left on the morning of 29 September 1825. Her cargo too had weathered well, and very little of the ninety-five ton load was found unfit for sale.

In the newspaper's 'Naval Inteligence' column John Gray went on to state that Captain Robertson's ship, the *Dexterity*, had been wrecked at Davis Straits, in lat. 72°N., and that the fishing so far, had been very poor.

The recovery of the *Active* was the talk of Peterhead for months to come, and marked a fitting end to David Gray's famous career. He retired from the sea that year, leaving his ship in his son's capable hands.

GREENLANDERS IN THE 'BLUE TOON'

An Inuit family came to Peterhead in 1825, probably the first of their kind to visit the port. As guests of the Grays their popularity spread quickly amongst the townfolk and it was a sad day for all when it was announced that two of the party had fallen seriously ill.

The Greenlanders could have had little resistance to the most common of complaints and thirteen year old Jacob Johannes and a woman known simply as 'Mary' both died in March 1826. Captain David Gray arranged for Jacob to be buried in the Gray's family plot at St Peter's Kirkyard. Mary was buried nearby.

Inuit (Eskimo) of Greenland, Sir John Ross, 1824.

'Scarcely a year passed', wrote Peter Buchan, 'without some ship or other being frozen in among the pack ice. Then the crew would abandon ship and bide in igloos along wi' the 'Yakkies'! Since the natives were very hospitable and since there were quite a few females around, ye could get a 'bidie-in' for the winter, nae bother ava!' *from 'Fit Like Skipper'.*

'As to their manners and common way of life, the Greelanders are very slovenly, nasty and filthy, and proper means to culture their minds contributes to their stupidity.

If there be any among them (as it will happen) who cannot work or get his livelihood , they do not let him starve, but admit him freely to their table, in which they confound us Christians, who suffer so many poor and distressed mortals to perish for want of victuals.' *Hans Egede, missionary in Greenland, 1818.*

THE GRAYS AND GEARYS UNITE

Captain David Gray saw his family united with that of the late Alex Geary when his son John married Geary's daughter Barbara on 18 December 1827 at the 'Muckle Kirk'.

For six years he watched over a growing dynasty until his tragic death in 1833. Captain Gray was fifty-seven years old when he took his grandson David fishing in Peterhead Bay for the last time.

ACCIDENT AT PETERHEAD

On Monday night, as Captain David Gray, accompanied by a little boy, was out in the bay, the boat was upset by the swell. The boy, fortunately, got hold of the keel of the boat, and clung to it till he was rescued; but Captain Gray endeavoured to swim to shore and had just got hold of the rocks, when he was swept back by the reflux of a wave and drowned. The body was not found until the next day. This melancholy event has occasioned general grief in Peterhead, where the Captain was long known as one of the ablest of whalefishing masters. His widow had but a month before, received the afflicting intelligence of the death of a son at Hamburg; and a few years ago two of her sons were drowned at Davis Straits.

The Aberdeen Herald, Saturday 6 July 1833

It is ironic that after surviving Camperdown and sixteen arctic voyages, Captain Gray should lose his life in such a way. He was survived by only two of his six children—Margaret and John. His other sons, Robert, David and George, died as young men, and his youngest daughter, Eliza, had died in 1825 when she was only nine years old.

Lilias Cowan, widow of the late Captain Gray, became the tragic victim of a fire at her Castle Street home ten years after her husband's death. 'Lily' was in her seventy-second year when she was buried at the Old Kirkyard on 16 January 1844.

THE *ALPHEUS, ACTIVE,* AND *ENTERPRISE,* LOST AT DAVIS STRAITS

John Gray took the *Alpheus* to Davis Straits in 1828 in the company of the *Active*, now with Alec Hutchison, and James Hogg's *Enterprise*. All three ships were wrecked that year, crushed in the heavy floe ice, but thankfully without loss of life. The skippers and crews were taken from the ice by the whalers who had managed to escape the worst of the freeze and all were safely home by the end of the season.

After the loss of the *Alpheus* Captain Gray was transferred to Kirkcaldy where he continued his career with the whalers *Hecla* and *Caledonian*. It was during his spell with the Kirkcaldy fleet that Britain's whale trade suffered its greatest loss of shipping.

1830: 'THE WRECKING YEAR'

Of the ninety-one whalers sent to Davis Straits from Britain in 1830 only seventy-two returned. Every ship had suffered damage, some quite severe, and of the ships that had survived the grim conditions twenty-one arrived home clean (without a cargo).

THE LAST TRIP OF THE *HOPE* AND *RESOLUTION*

The entire Peterhead fleet—thirteen ships—went to the Straits that year, with very poor results. Only George Simpson's *Traveller* (nine whales) and John Shand's *Gleaner* (six whales) made a profit. Several ships took two whales, others took one, and Captain Bill Walker of the *Commerce*, came home clean.

Peterhead's longest serving whaleship, the *Hope*, under James Volum, and Souter's 1814 record holding *Resolution*, now with Captain Tom Philips, were both wrecked at Davis Straits in the summer of 1830.

John Gray returned to Peterhead in 1836 to take command of the *Eclipse* from a retiring John Souter.

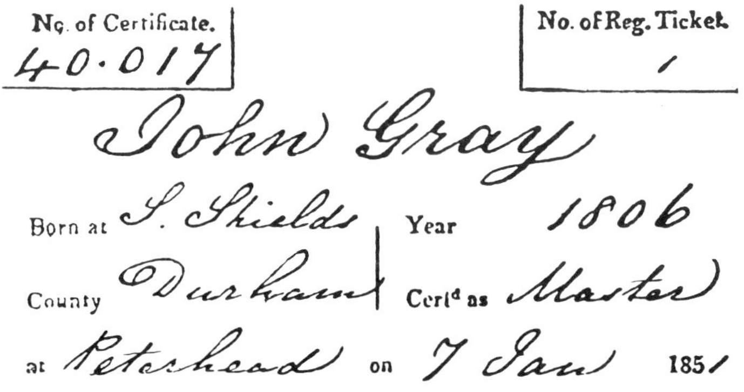

No. of Certificate. 40·017

No. of Reg. Ticket. 1

John Gray,

Born at S. Shields Year 1806

County Durham Cert^d as Master

at Peterhead on 7 Jan 1851

John Gray's Master's Ticket. PRO, Kew.

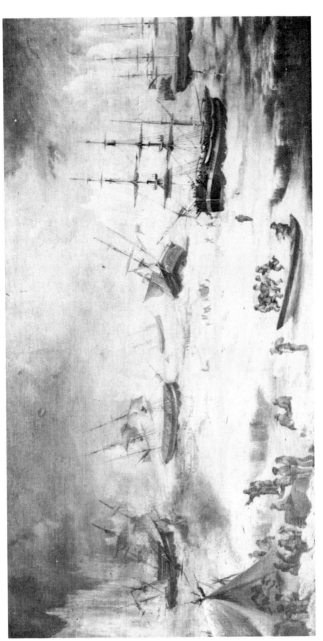

'Baffin Fair', 1830 (artist unknown).

'The ship wrecked mariners, nearly a thousand in number, were obliged to establish temporary abodes on the frozen sea. Their situation, though not desperate, was dreary in the extreme, yet such is the elastic spirit of British tars, that, as soon as the first shock was over they began enjoying themselves, exulting in the idea of being their own masters. Finding access to considerable stores of wine and spirits they transformed the rugged surface of the Arctic deep into a gay scene of festivity; some even gave it the name of "Baffin Fair".' *Discovery and Adventure in the Polar Seas and Regions*, Sir John Leslie, 1852.

THE PETERHEAD WHALING FLEET, 1836

At Greenland:
1 *Mary*   G. Arbuthnot

At Davis Straits:
2 *Gleaner*   G. Anderson
3 *Perseverance*   J. Ogston
4 *Traveller*   G. Simpson
5 *Eclipse*   J. Gray
6 *Resolution* (2)   J. Hogg
7 *Hannibal*   J. Birnie
8 *Union*   D. Cardno
9 *Superior*   D. Manson
10 *Commerce*   A. Stewart
11 *Joseph Green*   J. Volum

'VERY LAUDABLE CONDUCT'

The *Perseverance*, now under John Ogston, was lost at Greenland in May 1840. On his return to Peterhead Ogston wrote to the National Institution for Life from Shipwreck—an organisation founded in 1824 under the patronage of George IV which in 1854 became the Royal National Lifeboat Institution. His letter was delivered to a meeting of the Committee of Management on 9 November 1840. The following is an extract from the minutes of the day:

> Read the letter from Mr John Ogston of Peterhead, of 29th Sept, Master of the late ship *Perseverance* lost at Greenland in May last, stating that Captain John Gray and the crew of the *Eclipse* were instrumental in saving him (Capt. Ogston) and his crew of 45 men, by taking them off the ice and distributing them among the other ships to be brought home.—Write to Mr Ogston that this case does not come within the rules of the Institution, which is limited to cases of shipwreck that occur on the coasts of the United Kingdom—But, in consideration of the very laudable conduct of Captain Gray on the occasion the Committee has voted the 'Silver Medal' of the Institution to be presented to him.

Captain John Gray I, 1806-56.
'A smart and able sailor'.

The Greenland Sea Boys

The Peterhead whalemen were little versed in the niceties of sea-discipline, and apt to consider 'Jack was as good as his master.' To orders or inquiries the men responded briefly with 'Aye' or 'Nae'—the addition 'Sir' being quite unknown on the north-east coast. I do not mean to say that there was any insubordination on their part, simply a freedom and truculence of demeanour that was not often encountered on board the clippers. It was natural enough among the 'sea-boys' of a Greenland-man. There, among the ice-floes, the hazards of harpooning and lancing a whale, made rank as such of little account. A lubberly action on the part of an officer would be as disappointing or disastrous as on the part of a man. Instead of wages, each man received a 'share', and the skill or incompetence of each member of the ship's company was directly reflected in the pocket of each of his comrades. The fact made for plain-speaking and an entire absence of mere politeness.

On the other hand, in moments of emergency or peril, no more welcome shipmates could be imagined than the Greenlandmen.

Captain Andrew Shewan, *The Great Days of Sail*

'THE FOY'

As the fleet made ready for the north the harbours buzzed with activity both day and night. Traders and tradesmen of every sort reaped the rewards as the ships took on supplies and underwent last minute repairs. The whole town was involved; rope-makers, sail-makers, carpenters, coopers, stocking knitters, chandlers, butchers, bakers, blacksmiths, storekeepers, joiners sail-makers and wrights— everybody!—labouring through every hour of daylight.

By night the inns around the harbours swarmed with drunken sailors,—singing, dancing, cursing and fighting. It was the time of the 'foy', a tradition brought to Peterhead by the Dutchmen who used Keith Inch as a seasonal herring station in the early 1600s, and now avidly continued by the whaling boys.

In 1616 an enterprising Dutchman, who desired to enrich himself by ministering to the temporal wants of his countrymen, erected on the Inch, facing the South Harbour, a quaint looking tavern, which became known as 'The Crack'. ['Kraken'—a fabled sea monster.]

The tavern catered exclusively for Dutchmen, and there they spent their 'foy', or drink money, which was periodically paid out by the captains on behalf of the owners. Long after the Dutch had deserted the Inch, however, for a more lucrative fishing centre, 'The Crack' was utilised as a tavern. In 1760 it was occupied by John Sutter, vintner, and in the palmy days of the whale and seal fishing of the early nineteenth century, it still continued to do business. Within its walls, as in other taverns around the harbour, seamen were paid their 'foy', so that they could have one glorious convivial evening before setting sail for the Arctic regions.

Neish's *Old Peterhead*

As the young mariners drank their fill of porter and gin—from barrels labeled 'Knock Me Down', 'Flare Up', and 'Samson'—they found little shortage of female companionship, and no doubt in 'The Crack', the 'Ship' and the 'Black Bull', fair shares off the 'foy' changed hands during their brief liaisons!

RIBBONS AND GARLANDS

I was on board the *Oscar*,
A young and ardent dreamer:
Between those masts a garland hung,
With pennons fluttering free;
For every sailor's sweetheart
Contributed a streamer,
To bring luck to the whaler boys
Upon the frozen sea.
'The Ballad of the Oscar'

On the Sunday prior to sailing every ship was decked with flags and brightly coloured ribbons from stern to bow. The Muckle Kirk was packed for a special service of blessing the ships and crews bound for the polar seas, before the entire congregation, in time honoured tradition, made for the harbours to enjoy the vibrant spectacle.

The harbour was a splendid sight during the fleet's last few days in port. On sailing day local schools closed and great crowds lined the quaysides as one by one the whalers eased from their berths into open water, and in a blaze of colour made north and away from the cheering crowds.

We leave our sweethearts and our wives
All weeping on the pier;
Cheer up, my dears, we'll soon return,
'Tis only half a year!
'The Peterhead Whaler's Song'

HARPOONERS

Harpooners, more often than not the ships' mates, ruled the roost below decks. Not without good reason. Their journey through the ranks had been long and hard, as Captain William Scoresby explained:

'THE MODE OF MUSTERING GREENLAND SHIPS'

Abstract of the directions approved and transmitted by the Commissioners of Customs, for regulating the proceedings of Surveying Officers, admeasuring and examining into the State of Ships intended for the Northern Whale-Fisheries.

1. When the ship is completely fitted according to law, the master or owner gives notice that she will be ready for muster on a certain day; on which the proper officers go on board, when the list of the crew is delivered to them by the master, in which is described their names and stations, and they are all ordered on the quarter-deck when the muster begins.
2. The MASTER is called and examined whether he has on board a sufficient quantity of good and wholesome provisions, to serve the whole crew for six months with full allowance.
3. The SURGEON is next called and examined as to his abilities and qualifications. If for any reason he is rejected then a proper person is provided before the ship is suffered to clear out.
4. The HARPOONERS are then called and examined; those who have been three voyages in the character of boat-steerers, are passed; those who have not are rejected.
5. BOAT-STEERERS are examined; such as to have been two voyages in the character of line-managers.
6. LINE-MANAGERS are rejected unless they have been one or more voyages in the fishery.
7. GREEN-MEN are admitted provided they have never before been on such a voyage or fishery.
8. APPRENTICES must be above twelve and under twenty years of age when bound; and the indentures must be for three years.
9. The number of lines, harpoons, boats, and other requisities prescribed by the act, are examined.

The muster list is then made out, certified and delivered to the collector, who thereby clears the ship outwards, and grants her licence to proceed on her voyage.

Captain William Scoresby Jnr of Whitby (1789–1857)

LIFE AT SEA

The social gap between a skipper and his crew could not have been wider. Even at the highest polar latitudes, on the rare occasions when work was slack and the weather allowed it, ships' masters would entertain each other to dinner. At Captain's table the strictest rules of Victorian etiquette were religiously observed as guests enjoyed freshly shot sea-fowl, usually eider duck or diver, washed down with a fine claret, and followed by brandy, conversation, and perhaps a rubber of whist.

Below decks the scene was of course quite different. A persistent fog of tobacco smoke filled the crowded crew's quarters and gin flowed liberally. Shetland fiddles played as bawdy songs were bellowed out with passion.

'All Things Bright and Beautiful'

The 'whale-boys' were a rough-and-ready bunch, deeply superstitious, and God fearing to a man. A Sunday never passed without a time of worship, conducted in accordance with the Church of England's 'Seaman's Prayer Book'. Though very few of the crewmen were of that denomination, the custom was adopted in order that no favour be shown to either the Presbyterian or Roman Catholic company. With some ships having Divine Service both morning and afternoon, and Bible readings in the evenings, it was not unknown for the meetings to be abruptly interrupted by the 'blow' of a whale. Men would rush to the boats Bible in hand and, after slaughtering the poor beast, return to psalms and prayer.

SCRIMSHAW.

With its roots in the Inuit art of bone
carving and engraving, 'Scrimshaw'
became a popular pastime among
whalers. Images of whaling scenes and biblical studies were
tattooed into whale teeth and bones with a sailmaker's needle
and then darkened with a mixture of oil and soot.

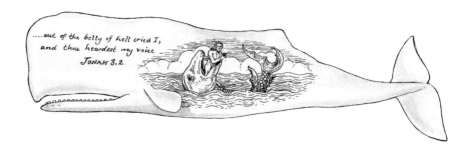

The Price of Success

The whale hunt brought great prosperity to the town, but there was a heavy price to pay. During the first half of the nineteenth century Peterhead suffered the loss of fifteen ships and many young lives.

The *Invincible* was the first casualty in 1822. The next was William Penny's *Alert*, though not on whaling duty. Some of the ships, especially after a poor season, took on general trade during the winter months. Penny's ship had come home from Greenland clean in 1825 and left for St Petersburg (in the company of George Simpson's *Perseverance*) in mid November. As the *Alert* left the Skagerrak, en route for London with a shipment of Russian timber, she struck rocks off Thisted on the Jutland coast. Though her crew and most of her cargo was saved the ship was smashed beyond repair.

The *Jean* followed in 1826. Captain Minto took his ship to the Greenland sealing with a crew of twenty-eight Peterhead men and twenty-three Shetlanders. They made the ice on 11 April and set about their work. A week later the gales that had plagued their journey north began to blow again but now with an awesome strength. After being pounded by gigantic waves for several hours the *Jean* began to take water. The crew suffered the frightful conditions huddled together on deck for nine whole days before they took to the whale boats and made south through the worst of the weather. They reached Grimsey Island, to the north of Iceland, after twenty-six hours in open boats. Four men had died at sea and thirty were by then in a critical condition. Two men later died during surgery on frost bitten limbs.

In August Captain Minto arranged for a Danish brig to deliver the Shetlanders to Lerwick and, for a fee of £300, take the rest of his crew back to Peterhead.

> They will long remember the benevolent inhabitants of that wonderful island of Iceland upon which they had sojourned for nearly three months.
>
> *Aberdeen Chronicle*, August 1826

The *Lively* of Whitby and the *Harpooner* of Bremen were lost with all hands that year.

In 1848 Captain James Lowrie of the Peterhead whaler *Hannibal* went down with his ship and all but one of her crew—Greenland veteran George 'Piper' Watt—when she was gale forced onto rocks off Norway. The ship had just completed her fifth season under Lowrie and was making for home with the crew of a derelict when disaster struck.

> Fast in the pitiless ice which tightens round her lies the good ship, her timbers groaning with the strain as though the vessel were instinct with life and feeling the thick ice—crumpled by the pressure like sheets of paper, and its broken edges rafting one above the other till there seems no escape from its overwhelming rush—every moment threatening to close over the shivering vessel and add one more to the list of the missing. All this time the crew, in spite of the darkness, cold, and blinding drifts, are working steadily at their posts striving to relieve the ship, or preparing for a hasty flight to the ice should the worst happen; yet so capricious is the weather and the motion of the ice that a change may come at any moment and the vessel be relieved from her perilous position. Or it may be that some of the crew are away on the ice; a gale comes on, and the heavy fall of snow obliterates their tracks and hides all the surroundings by which they could guide their course to a distant vessel; those on board adopt every means to indicate the direction in which the lost ones should bend their steps; but in the snow-laden and foggy atmosphere the fog-horn and beacon-light are useless, and when the dawn comes and a search-party is sent out great is the suffering which they are called upon to witness—frost-bite, madness, or even death. Add to this all the privation, hard work, and liability to accident, and the sealer is surely entitled to all his hard earned gains.
>
> 'Notes on the Seal and Whale Fishery'
> Thomas Southwell, 1883

THE NORTH HARBOUR DISASTER, 1849

On 10 January 1849, Peterhead was devastated when a massive storm breached the North Harbour's sea wall, and fifteen men lost their lives in the chaos that followed. One of the victims, Captain James Hogg, had in previous years survived the wrecking of no less than three ships at Davis Straits; the *Invincible* in 1822, the *Enterprise* in 1828, and the *James* in 1831.

William Boyd, a local solicitor, described the harbour tragedy in an account written the following day:

> Several of the whale ships broke from their moorings owing to the weight of water thrown in by the breach. Seamen were busy preparing new moorings when at nearly five o'clock, about half tide, a tremendous wave dashed through the breach, spreading over the quay to a great depth. The poor men on the quay were seen by those on board the ships—some running, others grasping the stones among which they were employed. Before this wave left them it was followed by another still more awful, supposed to be from 14 to 15 feet in depth, covered the men many feet deep, washed them into the harbour, which was now a boiling flood, and throwing with them an immense mass of stones.
>
> In an instant ropes were thrown from the ships and boats, and by these and other means many were saved; but we lament to add, no fewer than fifteen men perished. All the bodies were recovered, with the exception of that of Captain Hogg of the *Resolution*.
>
> The day will long have a place of sadness in the memory of many, and a general gloom has been cast over the inhabitants of Peterhead by the melancholy event which marked its close.

A worn and broken headstone in the south west corner of St Peter's Kirkyard recalls that fateful winter's day.

The Prince's First Command

David Gray was apprenticed in his father's ship, *Eclipse*, in 1844, and in the spring of that year made his first trip to the whaling grounds at Davis Straits. With help and advice from his skilful father David learned his trade well, and after only five trips was offered a post of Master of the whaler *North of Scotland*, a position he proudly accepted shortly after his twentieth birthday. Seven whales were taken on his first trip in command, more than his predecessor, a Captain William Allen, had captured in the previous three years. Gray's reputation as a 'lucky hunter' quickly spread far and wide and it was not long before the young Master was dubbed 'The Prince of Whalers'.

During long trips to and from the grounds Captain Gray studied his craft. He read everything he could lay hands on concerning the little known Arctic environment and kept detailed notes regarding tidal shifts and weather as well as carefully logged accounts of species he had seen. In a very short time Gray became an expert on the Arctic regions. His knowledge of such matters gave him a distinct advantage over fellow whale and seal hunters: not only did he often return to port with a good cargo while others struggled to break even, but he was also one of the very few whalemasters never to run aground or lose a ship.

ISABELLA GAMACK LAW

> Long time I've courted you, miss
> And now I've come from sea;
> We'll make no more ado, miss,
> But quickly married be . . .

Isabella Gamack Law, the twenty-two year old daughter of Peterhead merchant George Law and his wife Isabella Milne, became David Gray's wife on 11 December 1851. Three months later David left their Harbour Street home for what was to be his last voyage aboard the *North of Scotland*. He sailed from Peterhead in the company of his father's *Eclipse*, and, for the first time as a commander, his younger brother John with the newly commissioned *Queen*, a 379 ton schooner built at Birnie's Yard by Alexander Geddes for the Albion Seal and Whale Company. Also in charge for the first time were John Sellar of the *Gem*, David Ewan of the *Mary Ann Henderson*, and David Cowan of the *Spitzbergen*.

THE PETERHEAD WHALING FLEET. 1852
(all at Greenland)

	Ship	Captain	Seals	Whales
1	*Agostina*	G. Sellar	9852	
2	*Columbia*	R. Birnie	8167	6
3	*Commerce*	F. Henry	6125	
4	*Dublin*	J. Mackie	546	3
5	*Eclipse*	J. Gray	2925	5
6	*Enterprise*	W. Cardno	1944	
7	*Fairy*	R. Robertson	462	
8	*Gem*	J. Sellar	616	
9	*Hamilton Ross*	A.Wallace	8693	
10	*Intrepid*	R. Martin	4441	7
11	*Joseph Green*	A. Stewart	lost	
12	*Mazinthien*	P. Burnett	1262	3
13	*Mary Ann Henderson*	D. Ewan	6521	
14	*North of Scotland*	D. Gray	1912	6
15	*Pomona*	J. Robertson	5403	
16	*Queen*	J. Gray Jnr	2104	3
17	*Resolution*	A. Walker	5100	3
18	*Spitzbergen*	D. Cowan	lost	
19	*Traveller*	A. Hutchison	1076	7
20	*Union*	R. Walker	166	2
21	*Victor*	R. Martin Jnr	2773	
22	*Xanthus*	John Reid	7716	

The first casualty of 1852 was Captain Alec Stewart's ship, the *Joseph Green*. After twenty years at Peterhead the ship was wrecked in Greenland waters during the gales of 22 and 23 March. The incident was recorded in the log of Captain John Gray's *Eclipse* which for that season was being kept by John George Arbuthnot—'passenger on board'—the twenty-four year old son of local dignitary George Arbuthnot of Invernettie, ship owner and merchant.

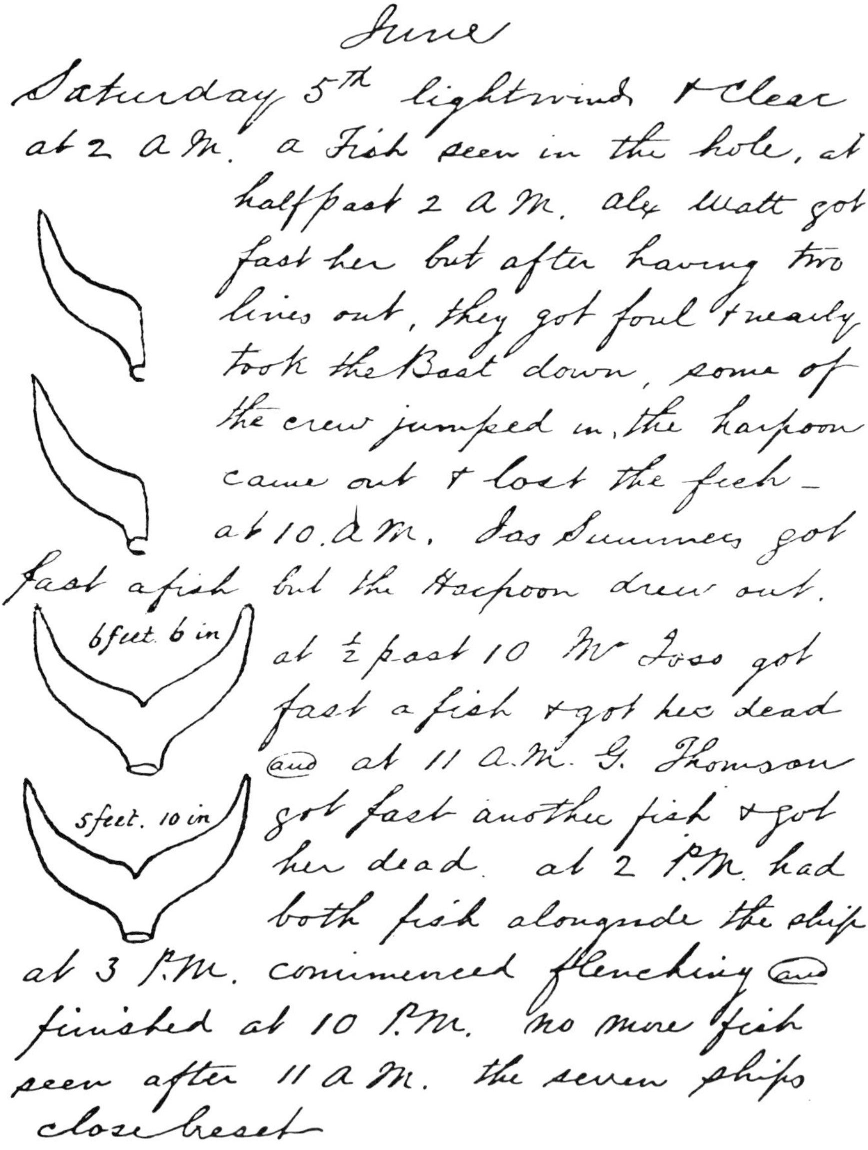

June

Saturday 5ᵗʰ lightwind & clear
at 2 a.m. a Fish seen in the hole, at
halfpast 2 a.m. alx Watt got
fast her but after having two
lines out, they got foul & nearly
took the Boat down, some of
the crew jumped in, the harpoon
came out & lost the fish —
at 10. a.m. Jas Summers got
fast a fish but the Harpoon drew out.
at ½ past 10 Mr Foss got
fast a fish & got her dead
and at 11 a.m. G. Thomson
got fast another fish & got
her dead. at 2 P.M. had
both fish alongside the ship
at 3 P.M. commenced flenching and
finished at 10 P.M. no more fish
seen after 11 a.m. the seven ships
close beset

6 feet 6 in

5 feet 10 in

Log of the *Eclipse*, 5 June 1852.
Kills were recorded in the ship's log by drawing a whale's tail; a half tail
marked 'one that got away'. Whale bone was measured at its longest
point and recorded alongside the capture.

Log of the *Eclipse*, 1852

Thursday 1 April:
Plying north of 'Jean Mayen' Island—moderate wind, showers of snow. Four or five sails in sight.
6 p.m.—Capt. of the *Union* of Phd. came on board, reported having been to the West Land [Greenland coast] and had spoken other ships, but had seen no seals. One ship reported to him the loss of the *Joseph Green* of Phd. having seen her water logged and abandoned—but knew nothing of the fate of her crew. She must have been wrecking during the gales of 22nd and 23rd March.

Monday, April 5th.
Strong breeze and cloudy. 8 p.m. Spoke the *Flamingo* of Hull—no seals —reports crew of *Joseph Green* all safe but the Master, having been picked up by the *Mazinthien* of Phd.

Later that same year Captain David Cowan and his crew had a narrow escape when the *Spitzbergen* was badly 'nipped' in the ice about thirty miles WNW of Hakluyt's Headland (North West point of Spitzbergen). Cowan's ship was one of several caught while searching for whales 'on the brand' (the floe edge) on 29 May, but as the others, one by one, got free, the ice around the *Spitzbergen* piled higher. For two weeks the crew laboured in raging blizzards to free the ship, but to no avail. With her bows stove and stern post twisted she was abandoned on the night of Thursday 24 June.

Captain Lee of Dundee's *Flamingo* reported to the *Eclipse* that she had seen the crew of the *Spitzbergen* making their way across the ice to the *North of Scotland*. She too was held firm in the floe, the Ensign at her mizen head signalling all was not well.

The following evening the *North* got free.

Log of the *Eclipse*

Friday 25 June:

2 p.m. Signalized the *Queen* and reported the wreck of the *Spitzbergen*. 6 p.m. Saw that the ice was slackening off.
11 p.m. Met the *North* coming out and got the Master of the wreck and 28 of the crew on board.

Saturday, 26th June.
We have learned now that the *Spitzbergen* had very severe nips on her at different times which had often lifted her several feet out of the water but the last had been the worst and it had twisted her stern post out and she filled with water.

Later a party of men returned to the wreck to recover the boats and what gear they could handle. The crippled ship was then ceremoniously torched and the shipwrecked men assigned to other ships.

David and John Gray sailed into Peterhead Bay on 11 September, and as the last barrel of blubber came ashore the *North* was handed over to a Captain Sharp.

Ship's agents, Alexander & Anderson, had commissioned Peterhead's leading builders, Lunnan & Robertson of Seagate, to build a new ship for David Gray. The 348 ton barque-rigged *Active*—named in honour of his father's first command—would be launched by the end of the year and ready for her first trip north in March 1853.

On Sunday 8 August, as *Eclipse* followed the Greenland coast south, a party of men were put ashore to capture walruses. Armed with his favourite fowling piece Arbuthnot joined the hunters for 'a welcome evening's sport'.

'Lat. 74°N 4p.m. Close in with the Great Pendulum Isle – two boats landed – got three sea horses, two white hares and some ptarmigans and partridges.'

The Maiden Voyage of the *Active*, 1853

Active, 'the smartest ship in the fleet', left Peterhead for Greenland on Tuesday 1 March—the last of the twenty-six ships bound for the whaling grounds that year.

John George Arbuthnot, a co-owner of the new vessel, accompanied David Gray that year, as he had John Snr a year before, and once more kept a detailed account of the voyage. His records survive today as the 'Journal Book of the Whale Ship *Active* in the Greenland Seas, 1853'. The writer begins his account in Bressay Sound, off Lerwick, when at six o'clock on the morning of 8 March, Captain Gray had the chief officer signal his complement of Shetland crewmen aboard.

> The vessels bound for the Greenland fishing leave Peterhead about the 1st of March and proceed to Lerwick for the purpose of completing their crews; the usual custom being to ship only the principal officers and boat-steerers in Scotland, making up the rank and file in Shetland. The vessels remain in Lerwick a few days, to allow the men time to get their clothes ready, many of them have long journeys to make on foot to bring their traps into town. At this time the men on board ship are busy in making everything secure to encounter the often very stormy passage to the ice. This will occupy about eight or ten days if the winds are favourable, but often takes three weeks or a month if the north-east winds set in with their usual heart.
>
> 'Habits of the Arctic Seals' Captain David Gray, 1870

Shetlanders and Orcadians had accompanied the mainland crews since the earliest days of commercial whaling. They were reliable men who suffered well the hardships of the polar seas. Agents in Lerwick and Kirkwall secured the whalers' berths, provided them with seal-skins and any other Arctic gear, and also arranged a credit system so that their families could buy provisions on account while the men were at sea. It sometimes took two or three trips before new recruits could return to the islands clear of debt, but at least they knew that during their long absences loved ones would be clothed and fed—a blessing in such times.

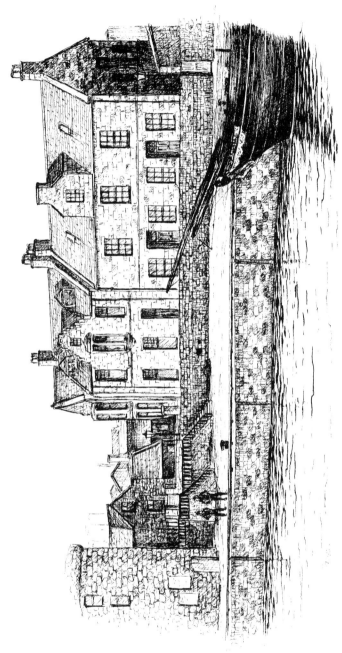

Active in the South Harbour, 1853.

The old Roundhouse, on the left, served throughout the 1800s as a Shore Dues Office and whalers' recruiting station. It was demolished in 1947 when the old fish market was extended to cope with a post-war rise in white fish landings. Only a few weeks before that the last of the Keith Inch Boilyards was demolished and cleared away.

The house on the right was the Customs Office for many years. The Gray's Harbour Street home was a part of that same building.

With tarry dress we'll reach Stromness,
We then shall go ashore;
With water less and landsmen scarce,
We soon shall take in more.
'Peterhead Whaler's Song'

The *Active* left Bressay Sound on 8 March and shaped a course for East Greenland. They made the ice at lat.74°30N, long.3°10W on Sunday 13 March, and fell in with several streams of 'young ice and slash'. All hands reported well. For the next few days the ship's company were busy preparing the stowed gear for the seal hunt. Several old 'Hood Seals' and 'a few Saddle-Backs' (harp seals) were seen on the ice, but none taken. Arbuthnot made daily references to 'energetic visits from Mr Frost Snr,' and on Tuesday the 22nd describes the ship as being 'snug in the frigid embrace of Mr Frost'. At this time all hands were involved in keeping the ship moving through the pack ice. As a group of men were engaged in sawing ice from the mast-heads to avoid the threat of the ship becoming top heavy and capsizing, others were at the bowsprit lifting and dropping an old whale boat onto the ice directly in front of the ship – a tried and tested way of breaking a way out known as 'milldolling'. Where the ice was thicker ice-anchors and ropes were employed allowing the deckhands to 'warp' or pull the ship through. Should the ship stick in the floe the crew would gather mid-ship and 'sally' her free—rushing from one side of the ship to the other until the ship rocked free. During such laborious times rations of 'Materia Medica'—tobacco and porter—were distributed freely amongst the exhausted men.

Though two old bladder-nosed seals were shot on the 2 April, sealing did not begin in earnest until Friday 8th. At 8 p.m. with a number of other vessels in sight, the *Active* lowered away six of her boats at lat.72°4N. They returned from the ice having taken 227 young seals. The following morning at 3 a.m. the boats left again, this time taking over a thousand seals. This went on until 4 May, by which time the ship had taken almost five thousand seals. The *Resolution* reported over six thousand, and the *Queen* little less.

Peterhead had sent twenty-seven ships north that year, taking a total of 98,201 seals.

Saddleback and pup.

THE FREEMEN OF GREENLAND

The 1st day of May is usually ushered in by the Greenland sailors, by the suspension in the rigging of a garland of ribbons, attended with grotesque dances and other amusements, and occasionally with ceremonies somewhat similar to those practised in 'crossing the line'. It affords opportunity for the display of feats of activity or strength; for the practise of such harmless frolics, as the circumstances of a whaling voyage will admit; and for the development of that species of original and extraordinary wit peculiar to the sailor.

Captain William Scoresby, Log of the *Baffin*, 1822

In the early hours of May Day the greenhands were taken on deck and subjected to a torturous initiation ceremony. Senior crewmen, masked and dressed in strange seal-skin robes, blindfolded the new hands, scrubbed their faces until they bled, and then shaved them with a rusty saw-like razor. A vile cocktail was then forced down their throats as a toast to 'Their Oceanic Majesties, Mr and Mrs Neptune'. The bizarre affair was thus concluded, and the new men were accepted as members of the 'Brotherhood of Greenland Freemen', the 'Honourable Fraternity of the Blubber Hunter'.

THE *ACTIVE'S* FIRST STRIKE

On Thursday 12 May the *Active* met with the Aberdeen ship *Superior*. She was making for home with her seal catch and Gray and his crew sent mail with her. The sealing was over and the *Active* was running north to the whaling grounds, the *Eclipse* and a Dutchman, *North Star* in close company.

The first whale was sighted at 12 noon on Saturday 21 May, as the ship patroled the floe edge at lat.78°36°N. Two boats were lowered and harpooner Andrew Falconer fired but failed to get fast. It was midnight on the 27th before the *Active* took her first whale, harpooned by Peter McDougal, a young ship's officer who would later become master of the whaling barque *Polar Star*.

Overleaf

Neptune and the Greenhand

'The proceedings commenced on the striking of eight bells at midnight. A sailor, strangely metamorphosed in a garb studiously extravagant, representing Neptune, ascended the deck over the bows of the ship.' Log of the *Baffin*, May Day 1822.

TAKING A GREENLAND WHALE

And now we've safely reached the ice,
We soon shall crowd all sail;
Each boat well manned with a strong band
For to pursue the whale.
'Peterhead Whaler's Song'

When a whale was sighted by the mast-head watchman his cry of 'A BLOW' signalled the duty crew into action. Two whale boats, each crewed by four oarsmen, a steersman and a harpooner, were launched, and the crew pulled hard towards the quarry—there was a bonus for the first boat there!

> The rowing cutters, all built in the 'Blue Toon' (Peterhead), were sturdy craft. To this day the fishermen along the coasts of Baffin Land and Greenland have what they call 'Peterhead Boats', faithful replicas of the whalers' boats.
>
> Peter 'Oxo' Buchan, *Fit Like Skipper?* 1985

In the bow the harpooner checked that he was free of the lethal whale line and braced himself for the strike. When close enough the oars were lifted and the harpoon released from the bow mounted gun. The whale would then 'sound'—dive for safety—the line running from its box to a depth of several hundred feet.

> John Milne told me that on one occasion, when he was harpooner's mate (line manager) in one of the whaling boats, his legs were caught by the line when the whale was fast, and he was dragged under water with the velocity of a cannon shot. He did not know how far he was carried under, but it must have been an immense depth before he got clear of the line. His bonnet came up first and showed the men where to look for him. When he did reappear, he came up close to the boat, so his life was saved.
>
> Frank Buckland, 1876

A crewman then hoisted the 'Red Jack', a stern flag to let his ship know the whale was fast. Cries of 'A FALL' resounded around the ship, and other boats were launched and raced to assist the striker. Sometimes the men who had been resting below decks made for the boats with no time to put on their seal-skins, the loss of a whale was a serious matter and far out-weighed the risk of frost bite. As the whale broke surface for air, after half an hour or more, the harpooner, with the wooden butt of his twelve-foot lance hard against his stomach,

pressed it home until the creature's agonising ordeal was over. The
lines were then hauled in, and with ropes around its tail the dead
animal was towed in triumph back to the ship, usually followed by a
great cloud of screeching gulls and fulmars. Sometimes a good many
miles were covered chasing a whale and the row back to ship may have
taken several exhausting hours.

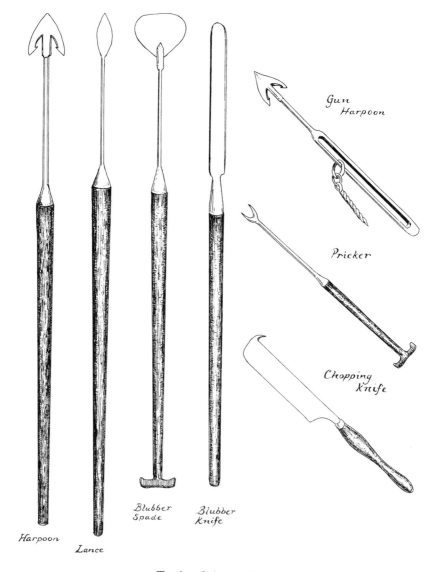

Gun
Harpoon

Pricker

Chopping
Knife

Harpoon

Lance

Blubber
Spade

Blubber
Knife

Tools of the trade.

AFTER THE KILL

The carcass was brought alongside the ship and chained to the hull for 'flensing' or 'flaying'. This was the process of cutting the blubber away, and was executed under the supervision of the officer in charge or senior harpooner—the 'specktioneer'. With metal spurs fitted to their seaboots the crew of the catch boat took positions on the whale's back and with long handled razor sharp flensing spades cut the blubber into strips to be hauled aboard.

The whalebone, or baleen, was taken from the mammal's mouth and the unwanted remains, the 'krang' cast adrift to sink. A few days later the blubber was 'made off'—brought on deck, freed from the skin and chopped into blocks. These 'horse pieces' were then put into casks and stored in the ship's holding tanks under the charge of the below deck supervisor, the 'skeeman'.

An average adult Bowhead (Greenland Right) produced about ten tons of oil which was separated from the blubber fats by 'trying' or boiling. Some of the larger American ships had on board tryworks but the Scottish fleet took the raw material back to quayside boilyards, in Peterhead's case on the 'Queenie'—Keith Inch. For weeks after the fleet's return the tryworks fouled the air about the town with a smokey stench as the oil was boiled from the blubber.

OIL AND BONE

The price of oil fluctuated a great deal but rarely made less than £30 a ton. Though sold mainly as a lamp fuel, blubber oil could be used in other ways. Dundee's jute industry, for instance, depended very much on regular supplies:

> This fat, unfortunately for Mr Whale, is very valuable, not only for burning purposes, but also for the dressing of jute, a flax-like material, which, when dressed with oil, assumes a lustre not unlike silk. With this jute are made carpets, curtains, and ladies' chignons. Jute is also used in the adulteration of black silk dresses.
>
> Buckland's 'Notes and Jottings'

In the early 1800s whale bone was sold at about £40 a ton, a price that rose to over £1,000 by the middle of the century. The keratin (fingernail) material hangs in strands from the upper jaws of the baleen whales, forming a curtain through which the Blues, Rights and Finners sieve their vast daily requirement of minute krill.

Winching baleen on deck.

All hands making off blubber.

The Right Whale got its name simply because in commercial terms it was the right whale to hunt. In addition to its good covering of blubber it carried about a half ton of whale bone, swam quite slowly, and, most importantly, it floated after the kill. The Right's fine baleen was used in a number of ways, from carriage wheel springs to umbrella spokes, and even found its way back to the job for which nature intended it—supporting blubber, but now in the form of plump Victorian ladies who somehow managed to force themselves into crippling whalebone stays.

Style – at any price.

The *Active* continued to fare well. On Friday 10 June another two whales were captured—this time by harpooners Andrew Falconer and John Simpson. The next morning Gordon McKinnon got fast to a 'fish', but when it was hauled up dead was found to have been previously fastened to the Dutch barque *Juno*, and of course, 'to the evident disgust of all hands, she was reasigned'. Monday the 13th saw another strike, John Thomson took a Right Whale as the *Active* dodged the ice-floe in the company of Burnett's *Hamilton Ross*. Peter McDougal struck again on 30 June, and Thomas Dowie yet again two days later. Dowie's kill was to be the last of the season for the *Active* but she continued to prowl the floe edge—'in some places as clear as the firmament; in others thick from the presence of a living mass of minute animal life'—for another whole month.

On Saturday 30 July, with her whaling gear stowed and studding sails set fore and aft, the *Active* bore up for home.

Two weeks later, with 130 tons of blubber aboard, she arrived in Peterhead where her captain enjoyed a double celebration—the new ship's faultless performance, and the August arrival of his first child, Isabella.

> And now in harbour safely moored,
> We next shall go ashore;
> With plenty o' brass and a bonnie lass
> We'll make yon tavern roar!
> To Greenland's frost we'll drink a toast,
> And those we love so dear;
> And across the main to it again
> We'll take a trip next year!
> The Whaler's Song

AN ENCOUNTER WITH POLAR BEARS

Few men have experienced the terror of coming face to face with a pair of hunting polar bears. Fewer still have lived to tell the tale.

George Martin, chief officer on board the Peterhead sealer *Xanthus*, had just completed an inspection of his watch—a party of men who were flensing seals some distance from ship—and was on his way back to report to his captain that all was well on the ice. He had walked only a few hundred yards when he came in among a series of ice hummocks that caused him to lose his bearing and steer a course away from the open pool of water where the *Xanthus* lay at anchor. It was then that the unfortunate man suddenly found himself in the close company of two 'ice bears', both hungry, and neither willing to let George go past. He turned slowly and began to walk away but the bears followed until the ice around him blocked his path.

Armed only with a flensing knife Martin survived for the next two days and nights by killing young seals and tossing the blubber to the bears that dogged his every step. The crack of distant rifle shot rang clear through the Arctic air as Martin's colleagues signalled their position, but he could do nothing to let them know he was still alive and in desperate need of assistance. He was frozen and on the verge of total collapse when at last the bears fell into a deep sleep. Wrapped in bloody seal skins to shield himself from the chilling winds he crept away, gradually increasing his walk to such a pace as his stiff limbs would allow.

Following the sound of the rifle fire Martin scrambled across the ice until he eventually caught sight of his ship. There he stood waving and shouting as best he could until the mast-head watchman returned a welcome gesture. All hands had given George up for dead, and the captain had already made the order to trim the ship for home. Safe once more in the company of friends Martin mustered what strength he had left and clambered aboard.

George died in 1867, while mate aboard Dundee's SS *Camperdown*, after losing his footing and falling into Dundee harbour as his ship made ready for Greenland. His injuries at first did not appear to be serious and Martin was taken aboard for the voyage north. He died within a few days of leaving port and was buried at Lerwick during his ship's brief stop over.

Overleaf

'He turned slowly and began to walk away, but the bears followed until the ice blocked his path.'

THE LAST VOYAGE OF CAPTAIN JOHN GRAY
'A smart and able sailor'

The year 1856 was a good one for the north-east fleet, but one of mixed emotions for the Grays. David's ship *Active* made port in mid July and John Jnr's *Queen* in early August, both with a good catch. The brothers' good fortune at sea, however, was not shared by their father.

John Gray had taken his ship to Davis Straits hunting the waters off Eclipse Sound, a seaway he had discovered at the north east tip of Baffin Island while running west through Pond's Bay in 1854. When the ship arrived at Peterhead on 13 September, Chief Officer George Murray delivered the sad news of his skipper's death. Captain Gray had died, despite the efforts of surgeon Elias Johnston, on 11 August after suffering heart failure. He was fifty years old.

> Mr Gray had been one of our most enterprising and successful whaling commanders, and has been master upwards of thirty years. Being bred to the trade under his father, Captain David Gray of the old *Active*, he has devoted his whole life to the whale fishing. In his career as Captain, he has invariably distinguished himself as father's son, a smart and able sailor and an expert fisherman. He has uniformly given the highest satisfaction to his employers, by whom he was regarded as a friend and gentleman.
>
> His remains were interred in the churchyard on Monday last, followed to the grave by a large assembly of sorrowful friends. His loss is deeply regretted by a numerous number of friends, and by all who knew him.
>
> *Aberdeen Free Press & Buchan News*
> Friday 19 September 1856

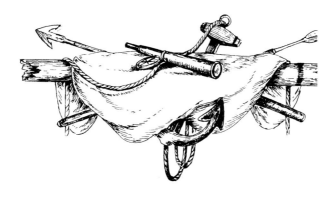

1857: The Summit of Peterhead's Ambition

The year of 1857 stands out in the annals of the seal and whale fishing industry as marking the summit of Peterhead's ambition in those days. When it is stated that no fewer than thirty-one ships left the port, carrying at least a thousands hands, some idea of the stir which the sailings caused may be formed.

Aberdeen Daily Free Press
Friday 27 January 1893

The fleet's finest year began with the launch of the 220 ton whaling barque *Polar Star* on Wednesday 14 January. Built locally by Stephen and Forbes she was placed in the charge of Captain David Ewan, late of the *Commerce*. 'It was an exceptionally fine day', according to the Buchan news, and 'an immense concourse of spectators cheered loudly as the ship glided into her future element in the finest of style.'

THE GREAT FLEET OF 1857

1	*Active* David Gray	17	*Inuit* J. Sutter
2	*Agostina* G. Sellar	18	*Kate* Joseph Scott
3	*Alert* D. Gregory	19	*Mazinthien* W. Allen
4	*Arctic* J. Reid	20	*North of Scotland*
5	*Brilliant* Capt. Alexander		Capt. Mackinnon
6	*Clara* John Sutter	21	*Perseverance* C. Brown
7	*Columbia* P. Allardyce	22	*Polar Star* D. Ewan
8	*Commerce* G. Arbuthnot	23	*Pomona* W. Robertson
9	*Dublin* T. Mackie	24	*Queen* John Gray Jnr
10	*Eclipse* A. Simpson	25	*Resolution* W. Bruce
11	*Elena* W. Sellar	26	*Sir Colin Campbell* D. Birnie
12	*Eliza* W. Abernethy	27	*Traveller* G. Brown
13	*Fairy* A. Taylor	28	*Undaunted* A. Walker
14	*Gem* W. Robertson	29	*Union* J. Stephen
15	*Gipsy* F. Hendry	30	*Victor* Robert Martin Jnr
16	*Intrepid* R. Martin Snr	31	*Xanthus* J. Cheyne

The great fleet's exodus began with the departure of seven ships on 9 February. Throughout the month they continued to leave in twos and threes for Bressay Sound where they would rendezvous with the fleets of other ports before heading north for Greenland. Peterhead's neighbour, Fraserburgh, was also enjoying its whaling heyday, although on a much smaller scale. Five ships left the 'Broch' (Fraserburgh) for Greenland in 1857.

February 9th:
The *Alexander Harvey*, Capt. Stephen, the *Enterprise*, Capt. Burnett, and the *Milenka*, Capt. Stephen.
February 23rd:
The *Sovereign*, Capt. Samuel.
February 25th:
The *Vulcan*, Capt. Stephen.

THE KRYOLITH TRADERS

Such a fleet could never last. The polar seal and whale herds had been plundered by too many for too long and now only the most skilful of hunters would survive.

Within ten years the great fleet was reduced to only nine ships. The *Gipsy, Undaunted, Eclipse, Traveller, Inuit, Empress of India, Fairy, Commerce, Resolution,* and *Dublin* were all lost within that time. The *Sir Colin Campbell* was sold to Norway, and the *Clara* to Aberdeen. Sellar's *Elena* ran aground at Shetland on her outward voyage in 1865. She was repaired at Peterhead and later joined a number of retired whalers in the kryolith trade, transporting ice blocks from the arctic pack for use in Victorian ice-houses and cold stores.

Other ships were put to work in the Baltic timber trade, an occupation which had hitherto been considered by whalers as a part time winter job, but now offered a lifeline to ship owners who were struggling to keep their businesses afloat.

Overleaf

List of Sailings from Bressay Sound. *Peterhead Sentinel*, 26 March 1858.

LIST OF SAILINGS FROM BRESSAY SOUND TO
GREENLAND, 1858.—We have been favoured with a
complete and accurate report of the dates on which
the Greenland vessels sailed from Shetland, and as it
will possess considerable interest to a large number
of our readers we give it entire. It will be seen that
many of the rumours which have been afloat regarding our vessels, have been altogether without foundation. Although the "Intrepid" and "Resolution"
had to put back, slightly injured, they were not later
in sailing than the majority of the other vessels :—

Active,	D. Gray	Peterhead.	13th Mar.
Æolus,	J. Hibb	Hull	2d ,,
Agostina,	G. Sellar	Peterhead	12th ,,
Alibi,	A. Stewart	Aberdeen	13th ,,
Alert,	D. Gregory	Peterhead	13th ,,
Alex. Harvey,	A Stephen	Fraserburgh,	2d ,,
Arctic,	J. Reid	Peterhead	13th ,,
Brilliant,	G. Alexander	do.	13th ,,
Clara,	A. Taylor	do.	13th ,,
Columbia,	P. Allerdyce,	do.	2d ,,
Commerce,	G. Arbuthnot,	do.	13th ,,
Chase (s.s.),	J. Gravill, Sen.	Hull	12th ,,
Diana (s.s.).	J. Gravill, Jun.	do.	12th ,,
Dublin,	T. Mackie,	Peterhead	13th ,,
Eclipse,	A. Simpson,	do.	13th ,,
Elena,	J. Stephen,	do.	2d ,,
Eliza,	J. Abernethy,	do.	12th ,,
Enterprise,	J. Burnett,	Fraserburgh	2d ,,
Fairy,	D. Carnegie,	Peterhead	13th ,,
Intrepid,	R. Martin, Sen.	do.	2d ,,

[Put back on 12th with loss of binnacle and
compass. Sailed 13th."]

Innuit (s.s.),	J. Sutter,	Peterhead	13th ,,
Kate,	J. Scott,	do.	12th ,,
Mazinthien,	W. Allan,	do.	13th ,,
Milinka,	J. Stephen,	Fraserburgh,	2d ,,
N. of Scotland,	G. M'Kinnon,	Peterhead	2d ,,
Perseverance,	A. Walker,	do.	13th ,,
Polar Star,	D. Ewan,	do.	13th ,,
Pomona,	W. Robertson,	do.	13th ,,
Queen,	J. Gray,	do.	13th ,,
Resolution,	W. Bruce,	do.	2d ,,

[Put back on 9th with loss of jibboom. Sailed
on 13th.]

Sir C. Campbell,	R. Birnie,	Peterhead	2d ,,
Superior,		Aberdeen	13th ,,
Swan,	R. Bushby,	Hull	13th ,,
Tay (s.s.),	A. Deuchars,	Dundee	13th ,,
Victor,	R. Martin, Jun.	Peterhead	2d ,,
Xanthus,	W. Cheyne,	do.	2d ,,

Lerwick, 15th March, 1858.

Peterhead Sentinel.

FRIDAY, July 2, 1858.

THE NORTHERN FISHERIES.

THE Elena, Captain Stephen, arrived here on Saturday from the seal and whale fisheries with 4600 skins and 70 tons of oil, and reports six whales caught up to the 10th of June, being one fish to each of the following vessels—Active, Agostina, Brilliant, Intrepid, North of Scotland, and Victor. The Perseverance arrived here on Wednesday with 2400 skins and 34 tons seal oil. Captain Walker reports the following foreign vessels :—Jan Mayen, 2400 seals, and Waleit, 1400 seals, on the 1st May, Martha, 2000 seals, on the 26th May; Maria, 4400 seals, on the 7th June; Ranger, 1000 seals, on the 10th June; Ice Bear, clean, on the 12th June; and the Sir John Franklin, 3100 seals, on the same date.

Traveller.

The career of this favourite ship can be looked back upon with pleasure. She was built in 1815, and was employed in the foreign trade for a few years. In 1821 she was converted into a whale fishing vessel, and that year sailed for Davis' Straits, under the command of the late Captain A. Hutchison. Her success has been varied, but, upon the whole, very fortunate, and well worth recording, and which we now print for the information of those interested in the fisheries :—

Year.	Master.		Tons Oil.
1821 to 1825,	A. Hutchison,	Davis' Straits,	635
1826 to 1838,	G. Simpson,	do.,	1971
1839,	do.,	Greenland,	39
1840,	do.,	Davis' Straits,	——
1841 to 1842,	do.,	Greenland,	68
1843,	Lee,	do.,	——
1844 to 1847,	G. Simpson,	Davis' Straits,	314
1848 to 1849,	A. Ogston,	Greenland,	114
1850 to 1854,	A. Hutchison,	do.,	405
1855,	G. Brown	do.,	120
1856,	do.,	Cumberland Sts.,	174
1857,	do.,	Greenland	28
			3868

From 1821 to 1834, the weight of a ton of oil was less than it is now, so that upwards of 300 tons have to be deducted to reduce the above to imperial measure. The value of her importations may be approximated at £200,000. She has been a mine of wealth to owners and underwriters, and though the latter will loose a few thousand pounds by her now, they cannot grudge it. The Traveller was a full built strong vessel, she stood many a hard squeeze in the ice, but firmly refused to yield when many of her companions were ground to pieces, and sank beneath the remorseless icebergs of the Polar Seas. After braving her last winter in the far north, and proceeding on her summer cruise, she was, on the 2d of May, swept on the rocks by rapid currents and wind, and became a total wreck, the utmost exertion was made to get her off, but she stuck fast, fell over on her broadside and was pressed down by a heavy piece of ice. Some provisions and other articles were recovered, but now the once stately ship, the terror of the Leviathan, lies a shapeless wreck on the dreary shore of the Polar Regions.

Peterhead Sentinel, 27 August 1858

LOSS OF TWO VESSELS AT DAVIS' STRAITS.

THIS week we received the unwelcome intelligence that two vessels had been lost at Davis' Straits whale fishing —the Eclipse of Peterhead, Captain Al. Simpson, and the Heroine of Dundee, Captain John Simpson. Both were lost on the 14th July. After having been considerably to the north, (some of the steamers were as far as Talbot Inlet, about latitude 77 deg. 20 min.) they were unable, in consequence of the ice to proceed towards Ponds Bay, the principal fishing ground. The passage was completely blocked up, and they were obliged to turn with the view of reaching the fishing ground by another course. They were, however, stopped by the ice, about latitude 76 deg. 30 min. (north,) and had to cut docks in the land ice. While lying there, a gale from the south-west, sprung up and forced the ice with such violence in upon them, that the ice in which they were "docked" gave way, and in course of two-and-a-half hours both vessels were totally wrecked. As soon as it was seen that there was no pros· pect of saving the vessels, captains and men endeavoured to escape, saving as much property as possible. The crew of the Heroine secured part of their clothing and their boats, but so suddenly did the Eclipse go down, that only two or three of the boats could be saved, the crew thus unfortunately losing all their clothing. The Captains were landed at Lievely, one of the Danish settlements, on the 26th July, and arrived here this week.

Peterhead Sentinel, 17 September 1858

TRAGEDY ASHORE

Deaths at sea and wrecked whale-ships were reported with cruel regularity, but nothing could have prepared David Gray for the misfortune he would suffer in the autumn of 1958. It was then, on the morning of 20 September, that his second son, David, died after a life of only fourteen days. A week later his young wife Isabella tragically shared the infant's fate, both victims of an infection contracted during the birth.

Despite these bitter calamities Gray continued as best he could. Before the captain left for Greenland, early in the new year, he appointed his sister, Georgina, as house-keeper and put his children, Isabella, Barbara, and John in her charge.

PETERHEAD.

Shares of Seal and Whale Fishing Vessel for Sale.

There will be exposed for Sale, by Public Roup, within the Office of ALEXANDER & ANDERSON, Solicitors, on TUESDAY, the 7th December, curt., at Seven o'clock, Evening,

SEVERAL SIXTY-FOURTH PARTS or SHARES of the Barque "KATE" of Peterhead.

Upset Price, £40 per Share.

For particulars apply to Messrs WM. SPENCE, or ALEXANDER & ANDERSON.

Peterhead, Dec. 2, 1858.

The value of a whaler, her stores, and fishing gear, were sold off in 64th shares. Merchants, shipmasters and traders spread their investments thinly – whale fishing was a risky business and a poor season could mean disaster for a speculator with all his money tied up in one ship. *Peterhead Sentinel*, 3 December 1858

Iron and Ice

Two matters of interest to the whaling community were covered by the *Sentinel* on Friday 4 February 1859. In a brief statement the Rev Mitchell announced that the traditional foy was to be replaced by an open meeting and soiree. 'With Mr Mitchell amongst them our sailors may rest assured that meetings will be at once interesting and profitable'.

The foy had been the highlight of the crews' year for as long as anyone could remember and, needless to say, Mitchell's declaration did little for his popularity.

'The Launch of an Iron Screw Whaler' headed the main story of the day. The mighty *Empress of India* was built at Hebburn Quay, Jarrow, by Andrew Leslie & Co., the largest ever purpose built British whaling ship. For two years the *Inuit*, the first of the iron whalers, had hunted the Greenland Sea, and though her early catch record had been unimpressive many whaling men saw in her robust construction the road to the future.

The *Empress* was a massive ship, described by the *Sentinel* as being of 'unprecedented strength' and 'perfectly impregnable'. With 100 h.p. engines, a blubber oil capacity of 600 tons, and a crew of over 100 men, she was the pride of the British fleet. After much deliberation her command was awarded to Peterhead's own Captain Robert Martin Jnr, late of the *Victor,* (son of the old *Intrepid*'s 'Oily Bob') 'a gentleman of indomitable energy whose great experience in the Arctic Sea well fit him for such an important command.'

An ode to the *Empress of India* appeared in the same journal a week later when an anonymous harpooner—McGcnagall?—wrote the immortal words:

> We hail this day! A noble ship is launched,
> *Empress of India* named,
> Which adds another to the fleet already so much famed.

The whalers left early that year, helped from their harbour berths to the open water by the Aberdeen steam tug *Heather Bell.* Spirits were high and the town looked forward to a good season.

By the end of February the whalers were well on their way north, and the town settled down for what was left of the winter. With no communication with the fleet, other than the occasional brief message brought to port by Shetland traders, it was an anxious time for families ashore. Only a few days after the last departure the first of the season's bad news reached Peterhead. David Geddes, a deck-hand on board the *Mazinthien*, had been swept overboard in a gale just south of Lerwick, adding another widow and two more fatherless children to Peterhead's list of tragedies, and setting the mood for what would be a sad year for the whaling folk.

THE *EMPRESS* LOST AT SEA

The *Empress of India* was reported lost by the *Peterhead Sentinel* on 15 April, only three months after her celebrated launch. Captain Martin and his crew had been picked up by Dundee's *Narwhal* in the Greenland Sea at lat.71°10N, 2°50W on 20 March. The rivets in her iron sheeted hull had contracted in an intense frost and the crew could do nothing to abate the sudden inflow of water. Though all hands were rescued the loss of the fleet's new flag ship had a devastating effect on the town.

More bad news soon followed, and when the *Inuit* came to grief on 2 April, her hull pierced by the ice, whaling's great iron dream became a nightmare. Her crew found safety aboard Captain Mackie's *Dublin*, and were later taken home to Peterhead by the *Dundee*, *Diana*, and *Resolution*. Peter Allardyce of the *Inuit* brought with him a letter from Mackie dated 14 May in which he described the conditions of the day as 'vile', and reported thirty-two of the fifty-four ships at the Greenland sealing firmly beset in heavy ice.

For the local worthies who had their faith and money so heavily invested in the iron whale-ships the season of 1859 had been a total disaster. Iron, the material that had given power and strength to general shipping, had been proved quite unsuitable for use in the Arctic's extreme weather conditions, and those who had subscribed to its polar introduction were forced to shoulder their embarrassing losses and think again.

THE Shipwrecked Mariners' Society has awarded the following sums to seamen wrecked at Greenland in the " Empress of India," and " Innuit" for loss of clothes, &c., through Mr Robertson, solicitor, Honorary Agent at Peterhead, viz :—George Martin, £2 7s. 6d.; George Murray, £1 17s. 6.; Andrew Catto, £1 10s.; Benjamin Buchan, £1 15s. Some of the crew of the latter vessel belonging to other ports, landed here, were also forwarded to their homes by Mr Robertson.

STEAMING AHEAD

John Gray Jnr left the *Queen* in 1862 and was appointed commander of the *Mazinthien*. At the time she was a sail ship but her owners had already made plans for her conversion to steam power. With the old rival Dundee now leading the field and using steam to great effect, the north-east could not afford to slip any further behind.

1862: THE RAILWAY COMES TO PETERHEAD

The opening of the Formartine and Buchan Railway's north east line, linking Peterhead to Britain's main railway system, brought great changes to the district. The practical boundaries which had hitherto restricted the area's economic growth suddenly disappeared and the potential for trade, both local and further afield was now at a premium. It was the time of the entrepreneur, a time when many made their fortunes.

Passenger travel was just as important. For the not so well off the local trains provided quick and easy transport around the district, and for families of consequence—such as the wives and children of successful whaling captains—the railway inspired a new way of life as regular trips to Edinburgh, Glasgow, and of course London, became 'quite the thing'.

The railway offered special rates to Buchan fishwives who travelled throughout the districts trading fish for farm goods – a welcome gesture of goodwill that helped keep the old custom alive for many years.

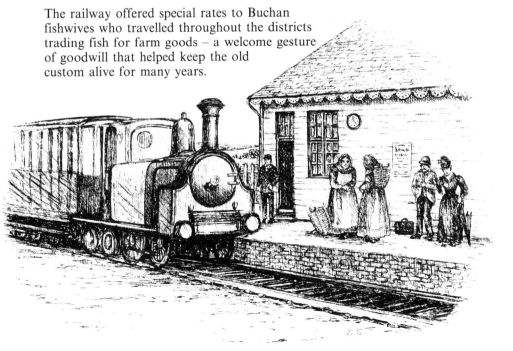

A BOAT CREW LOST SOUTH OF JAN MAYEN

In the company of the *Polar Star* and *Windward* David Gray took the *Active* on a double run in 1862.

With no success at Greenland, Gray made plans to head for Davis Straits and perhaps salvage something from what was quickly becoming a disastrous voyage. Gray had already lost eight of his crew when their boat capsized at lat.68°18N 8°W on 15 April. Three of them were Peterhead men, harpooner John Taylor, steersman John Fowlie, and George Watt, an eighteen year old apprentice.

The *Active* made for Davis Straits in mid June returning to Peterhead on 15 November with a meagre catch and a miserable tale to tell.

In contrast to the unlucky voyage of 1862, Gray found great success in the year that followed. After only moderate success at the April sealing the *Active* made north to lat. 79° where the ice was found to be in bad condition for whaling—jammed up in one tight pack, and held together by strong north-east winds. Gray saw no point in making any attempt to find whales there and resolved to make for the Davis Straits. As he came south and away from the pack-ice he encountered severe south west winds, and was forced, once more, to head north for the whaling grounds to the north west of 'The Island', Jan Mayen. There, on the morning of 11 June, he spoke with Robert Martin of the *Intrepid* who reported great numbers of whales in the area. The first whale was taken the following day, and by 12 August the blubber of fifteen adult Rights lay in the hold. An old harpoon was taken from the side of one whale, marked 'Pow & Fawcus' Newcastle Foundry, 1839'.

The *Active* left the ice on 14 August, landed her Shetlandmen on the 26th, and was back in Peterhead on the 28th with 170 tons of oil and nearly seven tons of bone.

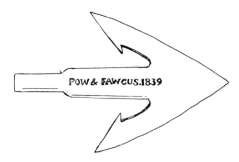

AMELIA WALKER
David Gray's Second Wife

On 11 November 1863 David Gray married for a second time. His wife, Amelia, was fourteen years his junior, the daughter of local land proprietor Robert Walker.

The Walker Brothers

Richmond House

Robert was one of seven children born to Robert Walker Snr and Jean Grant of Waulk Mill by Aberdour. After his apprenticeship as a cartwright at Rosehearty he and three of his brothers bought farming estates in the neighbourhood of Peterhead; Robert at Richmond, George at Balmoor, Alex at Grange, and Thomas at Howe o'Buchan.

The Walkers all had investments in the whaling fleet and its allied industries, and two of them—Robert and Alex—were connected to the trade through marriage; Robert's wife, Violet, being the daughter of Captain John Souter, and Alex's wife, Elizabeth, the daughter of ship owner John Hutchison of Cairngall.

In addition to his farming expertise Walker excelled as a botanist. He was a founder member of the Buchan Field Club, a society formed in November 1887 for 'the study of natural science and of the archaeology, folk-lore, history, and the literature of Buchan', and was also a member of the Parish School Board. In later years Walker partnered David Gray as co-owner of the Peterhead Rope Works.

CATCH POWER

In 1865 John Gray's *Mazinthien* and William Sellar's *Windward* were fitted for steam, a move later judged by some to have been the beginning of the end of Peterhead's whaling industry. The steamers, as Dundee had proved, were powerful and effective hunters with a catch-power that would quickly destroy the already struggling Arctic herds.

> Several influential parties have decided to add steam power to their sailing vessels, and it is more than likely that others will do the same; so that our ships may have the same chance of success as the auxillary steam vessels have which sail from another port [Dundee] What has prevented steam power from being made use of before this has been the fact that our vessels have all been built as sailing ships, and consequently their owners could not at once entirely afford to throw them to one side, which to a great extent must be done so as to allow steam power to be brought fairly into play.
>
> This, however, must and will be done, and I feel satisfied from the well-known energy and perseverance of our people that we will yet be able to keep this place in the pre-eminent position which it has so long maintained of being the principal port for the prosecution of the Seal and Whale Fisheries—the importance of which to this town and district cannot be overstated.
>
> John Brown, Buchan Seal & Whale Fishing Co. 1865.

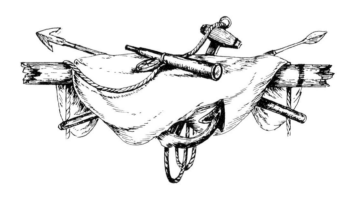

DAVID GRAY—A LIFEBOAT VOLUNTEER

More than 20,000 people gathered in Peterhead on Saturday 5 August 1865 to witness the launching of the town's first lifeboat. *People's Journal No. 1*, as her name might suggest, was gifted to Peterhead by subscribers to the Dundee based magazine whose generous donation of £800 had covered the cost of two 'self-righters'. *P. J. 1* was assigned to Peterhead, and her sister, *P. J. 2*, to Arbroath.

She arrived at Peterhead's new railway station from Aberdeen where, at the request of the *Journal*'s readers, she had been paraded through the city on the previous Tuesday. Vast crowds had come to Peterhead that morning, some by rail from the neighbouring towns and villages, and others by sea from Aberdeen aboard the steamer *Derwent*.

> Early in the morning flags were waving from every available point. The monument in Broad Street was gaily decked out with flags and two long lines of colours were hung across the Court-house green.
>
> The Lifeboat stood within the station enclosure on its transporting carriage, manned by its crew—twelve brave fishermen, with John Geddes, 'Sodger', as coxwain—men who, by their very appearance, sufficiently indicated the stuff of which they were made. Captain Robertson of the Lifeboat Institution was getting matters made ship-shape, instructing the launchers and explaining some part of his duty to one member of the crew. The crew seem quite at home in their position—looking so well in their uniform caps and cork jackets as to suggest the idea that they were old hands at the work. Everything is now ready, and Mr J. Reid, of the Horse Bazaar, appears on the scene with six splendid horses, beautifully and tastefully caparisoned, to draw the boat to the harbour.
>
> The procession, after the formal acceptance, started for the harbours, the Coast Guard and Royal Naval Reserve leading. Then followed the Artillery and Rifle Corps (of whom there was a splendid muster) which Bands played alternately during the progress. The boat with her Crew and Launchers followed the Volunteers, and the general public brought up the rear.
>
> ### THE SCENE ON THE PIERS—THE LAUNCH
>
> As the carriage was being unyoked and the launchers placed, the members of the procession and others who had accompanied them from the Station had time to behold and contemplate a scene which they assuredly never will forget. Never was there at one time such an enthusiastic turn-out of people in Peterhead.
>
> After an appropriate prayer by Rev Stewart, Mrs Colonel Ferguson of Pitfour (conducted by the Provost) stepped forward to the lifeboat,

and, smashing a bottle of port wine over her bow, said—*'People's Journal Lifeboat, No.1*—God Speed Her!' The cheers at this part of the proceedings were something really grand to hear, as the thousands on each pier took up the refrain making the air reverberate with their sound.

The boat was now rowed about for a time in the North Harbour. She sailed gracefully and easily; her crew keeping time like clock-work with the oars. Robertson stood in the stern of the boat—the interim coxwain, 'Sodger' Geddes, having the rudder in his charge.

The evolutions being finished, the crew were transferred to another boat, while the chain from the harbour crane was fixed to the boat in order to capsize her. The crowd seemed a little disappointed when they discovered that the crew were not to be capsized, but after all, this was rather much to expect, for the crew have probably many a good ducking before them yet: and therefore needed not to care for voluntary immersion. The calmness of the water is rather against the quick capsizing of the boat; but she is turned over slowly till her keel is uppermost. She remains not half a second in the position— righting herself like a duck, amid the renewed cheers of the assembled thousands.

The capsizing concluded, the out-door proceedings of the day terminated and the assemblage dispersed in as orderly a manner as it had assembled.

A public dinner, in honour of Captain Robertson, was given by the Lifeboat Committee, in Watt's Inn, at 5 o'clock.

Buchan Observer, Friday 11 August 1865

THE RESCUE OF THE *BLACK AGNES*

The new lifeboat's crew was made up of sailors, fishermen, and coastguards, and operated on a first come first afloat basis.

Captain David Gray was one of the thirteen volunteers who took part in an inshore rescue (the boat's second alert) recorded in the Life-Boat Journal, 2 July 1866:

On the 13th January the Peterhead life-boat *People's Journal No. 1* went off, and rescued the crew of three men from the schooner *Black Agnes,* of South Shields, which, while making for the harbour during a heavy gale of wind from the SSW, went ashore on the rocks near the entrance. The life-boat was reported to have behaved admirably on the occasion, During the service she was exposed to some very heavy seas, which severely tried her good qualities.

ROYAL NATIONAL LIFE-BOAT INSTITUTION.

[*Incorporated by Royal Charter.*]

Patroness.—Her Most Gracious Majesty the Queen.
Late President.—Admiral His Grace the Duke of Northumberland, K.G., F.R.S.
Chairman.—Thomas Baring, Esq., M.P., F.R.S., V.P., Chairman of Lloyd's.
Deputy-Chairman.—Thomas Chapman, Esq., F.R.S., V.P., Chairman of Lloyd's Register of Shipping.
Secretary.—Richard Lewis, Esq., of the Inner Temple, Barrister at Law.

14, John Street, Adelphi;
London, W.C., 2nd February 1866.

Dear Sir,

I am directed by the Committee to express to you their best thanks for your valuable services in assisting in the Peterhead LifeBoat to save the crew of Three men of the Schooner "Black Agnes" of South Shields – which was wrecked on the rocks off the South Harbour of Peterhead during a gale of wind on the 13th ult.

I remain,
Yours faithfully,
Richard Lewis
Sec.

Captain David Gray

A letter from the RNLI expressing 'best thanks' to Captain David Gray.
For their efforts the life-boat crew were each awarded ten shillings.

A few weeks after his lifeboat heroics Gray was once more en route for the Arctic, for what he later described as 'the most favourable season for whale fishing since 1856'. In a brief account of the trip, published in the *Buchan Observer* on Friday 20 July, Gray reported the other Peterhead ships, *Jan Mayen*, *Polar Star,* and *Kate* all doing well. He had not seen the *Columbia* for some time. The German vessels, the only other nation represented at the Greenland whaling that year, were also in fine shape; the *Flora* six whales, *Hudson* 4,500 seals and four whales; and the *Hanover* six whales. Gray also reported having seen several Norwegian 'sea horse' (walrus) hunters from the port of Hammerfest.

A temporary reprieve for a walrus herd as the Hammerfest hunters pass to the north.

One prominent reason for the success at the North whaling this season was the comparatively small number of vessels there, the fish not being scared as they would have been had more vessels been on the ground. The *Active* got the last of her 14 fish on 18 June, but did not get out amongst the ice till the 5th of July, having got beset.

The reporter concluded:

The *Active* in the meantime lies in the south bay [where she had been for three days] and is being lightened of part of her cargo before she enters the harbour—the tug doing good service in towing the *Alabama* out and in—the vessel employed at 'lighter' duty.

THE WEDDING OF JOHN GRAY JUNIOR

The Gray Christmas celebrations of 1866 began at midday on 20 December when Captain John Gray Jnr married Emily Lindsay of Montrose at Marykirk Parish Church, Kircardineshire. After the service the family returned to Peterhead by stagecoach where John and Emily made their new home at 14, Harbour Street (older brother David and his family were now living in nearby Jamaica Street)—overlooking the South Harbour and the streets of Keith Inch where the Gray brothers had grown up.

There the family would stay until the late 1870s when the Captain, his wife, eight children and two maids moved to the more spacious 'Clifton House' in Queen Street later the home of historian James Findlay, and a present day guest house.

Clifton House, Peterhead, 1880

SS *Eclipse*—'The Black Prince'

Feeling it necessary to keep pace with the times, although strongly disapproving of the innovation [Gray was of the opinion that whales would flee from the low throb of the engines] Captain David Gray had in 1866 the steamer *Eclipse* specially built for him. That vessel long and familiarly known among whalers of all nationalities as 'The Black Prince', was indeed successful, but it owed its wonderful success more to its able commander than to steam or any other improvements.

J. T. Findlay, 1896.

LAUNCH OF THE *ECLIPSE*

Steam Whale Ship of Peterhead

There was launched yesterday from the building yard of Messrs. Hall, a vessel of 555 tons builders measure, length 140, breadth 29, depth 16 feet, specially intended for the northern fisheries.

The ship has been built under the superintendance of Capt. David Gray, late of the *Active*, and is being equipped with machinery by Russel & Co.

Peterhead has hitherto kept the lead in drawing gold from the 'vasty deep', equal at least to that procured from California or Australia, and to a Peterheadian (namely a Capt. Wm. Penny), must be attributed the first suggestion of steam being employed in those regions. We expect from the enterprise of Captain David Gray, that the *Eclipse* will prove the precursor of many more similar ships, and thus keep alive, among our seafaring population, that daring and enterprise so absolutely requisite in such a profession.

Aberdeen Free Press & Buchan News, Friday 4 January 1867

The new steamer was named by Amelia Gray in memory of the late John Gray's famous whaler—the ship on which her husband made his first polar voyage as an apprentice sailor. At a cost of almost £12,000 she was the finest in the fleet, strongly built of oak, ship rigged and heavily fortified for ice work. Her engines could generate more than 60 h.p., she carried eight whale boats, and a crew of fifty-five.

SS *Eclipse* in the Greenland ice.

Few people have any idea of the dangers incurred by whalers in the
Arctic Seas. The ships are built exceedingly strong, and necessarily so,
for the work they have to do is perilous.

About forty feet of her, outside, from the stem, is, as it were, double
armoured with an amazing thickness of oak planking and iron bolted
together in the manner which experience proves is best for fighting ice.
The cut-water is iron, forming a very sharp wedge to split the ice. Woe
betide any ship that collides with her!

The Eclipse Whaling Ship, Frank Buckland

With the Aberdeen harbour ceremony over, the ship's builders took
her owners, captain and guests to luncheon, after which the party
boarded the train for Peterhead where the celebrations continued over
dinner at Watt's Inn.

Progress on the fitting of Gray's new ship almost came to a stand
still at the end of the month as the north east suffered its heaviest snow
storm since 1837, closing down the Peterhead railway for several days.

Perfect in every detail, this 1:48 scale model of SS *Eclipse* was made by Captain Gray's youngest son, James, for the Royal Museum, Edinburgh.

She was nevertheless ready on schedule and on 6 March 1867 SS *Eclipse* made for the open sea off Aberdeen in a strange mid-morning twilight. The sudden eclipse of the sun came as a shocking surprise to most of the crew and spectators—but not of course to her captain and owners who had planned the spectacular event many weeks before.

On her way north she called at Peterhead Bay where she signalled ashore that all was well before pulling once more into open water and shaping for Lerwick.

Though every step had been taken to ensure the ship's efficiency little effort was made to make life easier for her crew. 'I had the curiosity', one of her foc'sle hands later wrote, 'to measure my bunk and find it 2ft 4ins high, 6ft long and 3ft broad; made to hold myself and one other twice my size. Bunks generally held three in them, some four—but of course some of the men were in different watches. But a mighty squash it was when it was all hands in!'

The SS *Eclipse* went on to become a legend at Peterhead, as did her sister ship *Hope*. Built six years later for Gray's brother John, the *Hope* first sailed for Greenland on 4 March 1873. She was home from the sealing only seven weeks later, a 'full' ship. It is quite common for a ship to be named after a child, but in the case of one of John Gray's children the situation was reversed. The captain's second son was baptized John 'Hope' Gray in 1877.

To accompany the ship, Gray made a 1:16 model of a whale boat of the Peterhead type from that same era. These boats were carvel built with brass sheathing on their bows. Generally about 27 feet long, each boat carried six men including a harpooner and steersman. Although the bow-mounted swivel gun was introduced in the early 1800s, the hand-held 'harp-iron' remained an integral part of a boat's gear.

A new type of harpoon head was patented by Robert Tindall Jnr of Fraserburgh in July 1858. His invention made use of expanding barbs, designed to increase the weapon's penetration depth and holding power.

TRAUMA AT DAVIS STRAITS

The Hull whale ship *Diana* back from the Straits where she had been beset during the winter. The captain and eleven men are dead and about thirty men disabled.

Robert Walker's Diary, 8 April 1867

The *Diana* was caught in the ice at Frobisher Straits in September 1866. The last ship to see her was Peterhead's *Intrepid*, a ship that had been beset alongside her for several days but luckily found a way south and away from the worst of the ice.

The luckless ship began her torment with a crew of fifty-five men but after suffering a dreadful Arctic winter made Shetland with only five men fit for duty. Some had died and many lay dying. The ship, battered and ice-crushed, was in a terrible state. Her boats had long since been broken for firewood, as had every spar of wood above and below deck, as the men fought to stay alive through the bleak winter months of darkness.

. . . the sight which met the eyes of the people who first boarded her cannot well be told in prose. Dante might have related it to the 'Inferno'. Coleridge's 'Ancient Mariner' might have sailed in such a ghastly ship—a charnel-house not to be described.

Peterhead Sentinel, Friday 12 April 1867

One of the more able survivors told of how the crew had left their ship and made camp on the ice so that they might manage some sleep away from the deafening creaking and groaning of the crushed timbers, only to be forced back on board by the insufferable cold. As rations came to an end many of the miserable scurvy-stricken, dysentry worn men slowly began to lose their minds. With no tobacco some smoked what was left of the tea and coffee—madness and death surrounded the few who had somehow managed to keep their wits about them.

Most pitiable sights of all [recalled one witness], were the ship's boys, with their young faces wearing a strange aged look not easily to be described.

DR ROBERT GRAY

David Gray's son Robert first sailed aboard the *Eclipse* in 1883. He became first officer aboard his father's ship and served with him until 1890. On 22 April 1888, while on duty at Greenland, Robert rescued a shipmate from the frozen seas, an act of bravery for which he was awarded the Albert Medal.

He went on to study medicine, and on graduation from Aberdeen University Robert left for Assam to join his twin brother William, by now a successful tea planter.

'Bob' served there as a Medical Officer for some time before marrying Hilda Mummery, *c*.1912. (Hilda was the daughter of the English mountaineer who lost his life during an attempt on Nanga Parbet in 1895.) The doctor and his family later settled in Devon from where he continued to practice, sometimes as a ship's surgeon and sometimes ashore.

He wrote at length about his whaling experiences, his notes appearing in many publications including *The Scottish Naturalist* magazine and *The Transactions of the Buchan Field Club*. His expertise in such matters was later acknowledged by Encylopedia Britannica when he was invited to prepare a whaling report for its ninth edition.

Suffering from cancer, Dr Gray committed suicide in 1940. he was 76 years old.

Not every voyage made by David Gray and the *Eclipse* was a success as Dr Gray later explained in an article for *The Scottish Naturalist* in January 1933.

> The season of 1868 was a very open one; the edge of the ice lay far west with much open water between it and the land, and according to my father 'there was only food for the whales in ice-free water'.
>
> Very few whales were seen and only three caught; all small and all at the northern fishing [beyond Lat.76°N]. The *Eclipse* returned in September with only 25 tons, the produce of three whales and a few seals. Her balance sheet, which shows a loss of £1,217, shows payments amounting to £2,146 (viz., wages, £871; provisions, £629; coals, £220; general charges, £424;) and receipts amounting to £928 (viz., oil sold less oil money to crew at £7 per ton and boil-yard expenses at £1 per ton, £556; whale-bone, less crew's bone-money, £316; sealskin less crew's skin money, £55). In the balance sheet the vessel is valued at £12,347.

What was lost at sea was gained ashore in the summer of 1868, as Robert Walker's diary recalls:

July 21. The warmest day ever known in this country, at Wimbledon
Meeting. 128° in the sun.

Sept. 2nd. This has been the finest harvest I have ever seen and the
earliest unless 1826.

Eclipse from Greenland with about 25 tons.

Robert Walker Gray (with Winchester sealing rifle) on board SS *Eclipse*
with his father, 1888.

'A characteristic feature of whaling ships is the masthead, or crow's nest [invented by Captain William Scoresby *c.1800*]. From this lofty vantage point the ship was conned while in the ice, and for this purpose, in some ships, a compass was fixed to the main truck, and communication maintained with the engine room by means of a bell or signalling device. The masthead was also used for the purpose of looking out for whales and seals.' James Gray, *Mariner's Mirror*, Vol 23, 1937.

The captain to the topmast has gaen,
Wi' the spyglass in his han',
A whale, a whale, a whale cried he,
And she blows at every span brave boys,
And she blows at every span!
'The Greenland Song', Trad.

SMALL-POX AND FEVER

On 24 February, 1872, the harbour authorities received a telegraph from the Shetlands warning of an outbreak of small-pox and fever in Lerwick town. The old Roundhouse, Peterhead's South Harbour mustering station, set about the business of signing extra hands for the ships now forced to sail to the fisheries without their usual compliment of islanders.

Lerwick's temporary isolation meant further complications for the fleet. The well established stop off point provided crews an opportunity to take on fresh water and sand ballast, fix the 'hurricane house' (the crow's nest barrel) at the mast head, and trim the ship for a stormy passage to the ice barrier.

Necessity ensured that all problems were resolved and SS *Eclipse* left port for Greenland on 6 March—only a few days later than planned—for what was to be a most famous voyage.

> The year 1872 is remarkable by one extraordinary circumstance. While the rest of the ships pursued the even tenor of their course, and frequented the same grounds in quest of whales and seals, Captain David Gray went for 'pastures new', with the result that while he got no seals—as a matter of fact he did not want them, flying for higher game—he succeeded in getting on board the produce of no fewer than fifteen whales, landing in Peterhead the biggest shipload of oil and bone that ever has come to the country. The *Eclipse* was indeed 'full ship' having in her hold 220 tons of oil, besides whale bone.
>
> *Aberdeen Daily Free Press*, 9 February 1893

After taking three whales at the 'northern' fishing, off Hakluyt's Head, the *Eclipse* left the other five Peterhead ships and made for what was known as the 'southern' fishing, the grounds south of latitude 76°N. Twelve whales were killed bringing the ship's catch up to a record 235 tons of oil and eleven tons of bone.

> The *Eclipse* was unable to reach the ground from the N.E.—the usual route—but after coming out east and turning a point succeeded in reaching it from the S.E. She made most of the captures about the end of July about lat.72°, long.14°W., near a very large and thick unbroken floe. Harpoons were found in 3 of the whales she caught: two were old and not capable of being identified, but one belonged to the *Alibi* of Peterhead and had been fired into the animal only a year before.
>
> Dr Robert Gray, *The Scottish Naturalist*, 1933

As *Eclipse* approached Peterhead harbour on 14 August, the jubilance of her crew was marred by the sudden death of their most senior member, James Webster. He was seventy-five years old and had been a Greenland regular since his first trip north in 1815!

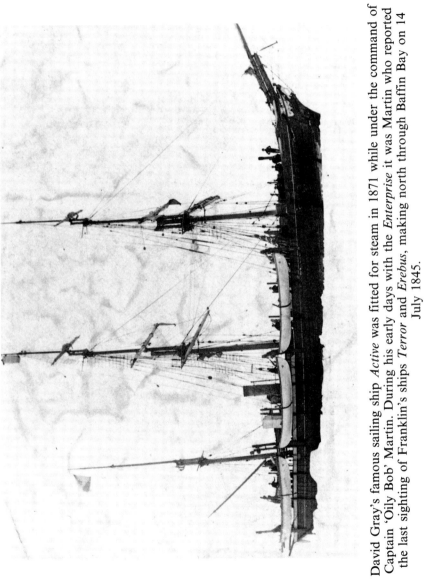

David Gray's famous sailing ship *Active* was fitted for steam in 1871 while under the command of Captain 'Oily Bob' Martin. During his early days with the *Enterprise* it was Martin who reported the last sighting of Franklin's ships *Terror* and *Erebus*, making north through Baffin Bay on 14 July 1845.

Seal and Whale Fishing Steam Ship
FOR SALE, AT PETERHEAD.

There will be Exposed for Sale, by Public Roup, within
LAING's HOTEL, Peterhead, on FRIDAY, 8th August
next, at One o'clock Afternoon, if not previously dis-
posed of by Private Bargain,

ALL and WHOLE, the S.S. Whale Ship
"ACTIVE," of Peterhead, as she pre-
sently lies in the North Harbour there,
with her Stores, Appurtenances, and Fishing Gear.

The s.s. "Active is of the burthen of 236 tons N.M.,
and 380 tons O.M. per Register, was built at Peterhead,
as a sailing vessel, expressly for the prosecution of the
Seal and Whale Fisheries, and in 1871 was converted into
a Screw Steamship, and equipped with Oil Tanks, &c., so
that this vessel is in every way suitable for prosecuting
the trade in which she has been employed. Sails fast,
and answers in all respects under canvas, with or without
steam; has been efficiently kept up; is in most excellent
order, both as regards Hull, Spars, and Rigging; is well
found in Stores, only requiring Provisions to proceed on
another voyage.

For further particulars, apply to JOHN BROWN, Esq.,
the Owner.

St Andrew Street,
Peterhead, 24th July, 1873.

Active for sale, *Peterhead Sentinel*, 6 August 1873.

---

facing page
Shipping blubber, and Narwhal on deck.

3 July: 73°N, 14°13′W. 'Caught a narwhal, 15 feet 1 inch in length; 9 feet
5 inches in girth, tusk 7 feet 6 inches in length.' Captain Gray's log, SS
Eclipse, 1877.

THE STORM OF 1876

In October 1876 the *Eclipse* was taken to Aberdeen for new engines. As she lay in the safety of dry-dock a storm of unprecedented force struck the east coast.

> Not within the memory of man has there been such a destruction of life and property on our coast as within the last few days. The continued easterly gales came to a high yesterday at night accompanied with snow and lightning. There are twenty ships wrecked between Ythan and Stonehaven and as bad at other places along the coast. There is one ship wrecked at Boddom, one at Salthouse Head, one at the Kirkshore, one at Scotston, one at Annachie, one at Rattray, and one at Cairnbulg. Some of them large ships and most of them Danish or Norwegian. It is unknown now how many may have foundered at sea, the whole coast is strewn with wreckage. It is believed that 300 lives have been lost on the east coast. Today three disabled ships have been brought into Peterhead. Inland there is a severe snow storm and trains have been stopped on all the lines.
>
> Robert Walker's Diary, Christmas Eve, 1876

> Heaviest snow since 1838 – still falling.
> Measles still raging in Peterhead,
> Fifteen children buried in one day.
>
> Robert Walker's Diary, Christmas Eve, 1878

'A DOCTOR AT SEA'

For the voyage of 1880 Captain John Gray Jnr employed the services of a young medical student from Edinburgh. His name, Arthur Conan Doyle, of course meant little at the time: he was in fact best known to those aboard the *Hope* as the 'Great Northern Diver', a name given to him by the crew after he had fallen into the icy seas for a record third time.

'The Great Northern Diver'.

He was determined to succeed as a whaler and carried out even the most elementary duties with a keen interest. Although as surgeon Doyle was not expected to take part in the hunting he insisted in taking his turn at the oars of the catch boats, reflecting on one such occasion in an article for the *Idler*, in 1892.

> Yet amid all the excitement—and no one who has not held an oar in such a scene can tell how exciting it is—one's sympathies lie with the poor hunted creature. The whale has a small eye, little larger than that of a bullock, but I cannot easily forget the mute expostulation which I read in one, as it dimmed over in death within hand's touch of me. What could it guess, poor creature, of laws of supply and demand, or how could it imagine that when nature placed an elastic filter inside its mouth, and when man discovered that the plates of which it was composed were the most pliable and yet durable things in creation, its death-warrant was signed.
>
> 'The Glamour of the Arctic' A.C.D.

Doyle had a deep respect for his captain and in his memoirs he wrote
of John Gray:

> I should have found it intolerable if the captain had been a bad fellow,
> but John Gray of the *Hope* was really a splendid man, a grand seaman
> and a serious-minded Scot, so that he and I formed a comradeship
> which was never marred during our long tête-à-tête. I see him now, his
> ruddy face, his grizzled hair and beard, his very light blue eyes always
> looking into far spaces, and his erect muscular figure. Taciturn,
> sardonic, stern on occasion, but always a good just man at bottom.

Captain Gray was impressed by his doctor's efforts at sea, so much so
that he offered him a second trip, on double pay, as surgeon-
harpooner. Though flattered by his skipper's generous invitation,
Doyle respectfully declined.

His Greenland voyage was an unforgettable experience that would
later serve the young writer well.

> It directly supplied inspiration for his first two really good stories, 'The
> Little Square Box', and the 'Captain of the Pole Star'. It was the sea
> which discovered the literary genius of Arthur Conan Doyle.
>
> Owen Dudley Edwards

The crew of SS *Hope* outside the Boilyards, Keith Inch, *c.*1880.

'THE SEA HORSE AND THE UNICORN'

By the year 1880 the Greenland Right Whale was a rare sight in the northern seas, and in order to make their voyages worthwhile the Peterhead skippers were forced to turn their attention to 'lesser game'.

The 'Seahorse'.

Smaller species—Odonoceti or toothed whales—had been taken in small numbers for many years but were now hunted, along with seals and walrus—the sailor's 'Sea Horse'—in hope that the mixture might raise enough money at sale to make the trip worthwhile. Even polar bears, which had in the past been shot for sport, were now being skinned for the fur trade, or taken alive for sale to zoological gardens. The going price for a healthy adult female was £35 in 1880.

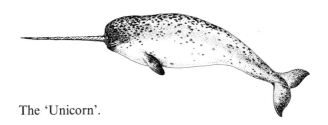

The 'Unicorn'.

The Bottlenose Whale, Beluga or White Whale, and the Narwhal, had no baleen but were of great value to the whaler as, in addition to their blubber fat, they carried skull spermaceti—a fatty, brittle, semi-transparent matter known to whalers as 'whale-shot', and used in the manufacture of candles and a variety of strange Victorian ointments. The tusk of the Narwhal, the whaler's 'Unicorn', was also highly prized and sold at twenty to thirty shillings a pound. Much of this 'high grade' ivory was sent to Japan and China where it was carved and used to decorate places of worship. Little of the Unicorn was wasted, even its inner skin was sold for shoe leather, and, in earlier years, the tusks were often sold as those of a genuine unicorn!

Though hunted with a vengeance by the Norwegians the walrus escaped the serious attention of the home fleets. Those that were taken by the Peterhead ships provided good quality blubber, but more importantly the tusks of the male, which were often more than two feet long, provided dentists with an ivory they considered ideal for the manufacture of false teeth.

The native Inuit tribes of the polar regions had hunted the walrus for generations. The animals were very much a part of their tribal culture and folklore and were often featured in paintings and ivory tusk carvings. The killing of a walrus was a milestone in the career of a young hunter and was cause for celebration among his family and friends. Spearing an adult animal was a dangerous undertaking, and should the hunter miss his mark—at the back of its head—the walrus could turn on his enemy's kayak, and tear it to pieces. Many hunters lost their lives in this way.

The Greenlanders taught visiting whalers how to use the walrus to best advantage. Nothing was wasted. The meat was eaten, the skins stretched and used for clothes and bedding, and even its intestines were washed out and filled with the dead animal's blood to make a kind of sausage.

Making off walrus skins.

'BOTTLENOSING'

> They are very unsuspicious, coming close alongside the ship, round
> about underneath the boats, until their curiosity is satisfied . . . They
> can leap many feet out of the water, even having time to turn their
> heads and look about them, taking the water head first, and not falling
> into it sideways like the larger whales.
>
> Captain David Gray, '*Proceedings of the Zoological Society*,' 1882

Interest in the bottlenose whale began in Peterhead in 1877, when the
Jan Mayen, having missed the seals, brought ten into port. They grew
to a length of thirty feet and yielded about two tons of oil, which was
soon found to be on a commercial par with that of the Right whale. It
was after this discovery that the slaughter of the bottlenose began in
earnest.

Bottlenose whale.

The year 1882 was a record one at the 'bottlenosing'; the fleet took
463 whales with more than 200 falling to David Gray's *Eclipse* (the
species' interest in ships and habit of swimming alongside injured
companions often resulted in many herd members being killed at one
time). They were taken at Greenland during the months of May and
June, and in order to accommodate his vast 230 ton cargo Gray saw to
it that all surplus coals and stores were thrown overboard. Even the
bread was removed from its tank and stored in lockers to make way
for blubber.

When the *Eclipse* arrived home on 5 July she was indeed 'full ship',
and with oil now at £60 a ton her company could not have been in
finer spirit!

Practical Natural History.

AFTER THE WHALES AND YOUNG SEALS.

June 29.—Light wind from south, with thick fog until 9 p.m., when it cleared away and we had a very fine night. The edge of the ice just visible from the bridge. Killed five whales, flenched them, hoisted the boats up and put the engines on half-speed for home, having now as much cargo as the ship can hold.

June 30.—Light winds throughout, the ship going steadily onwards. All hands employed in cleaning up and in putting the whaling gear away.

The following table shows the number of shots fired, of whales taken and lost :—

Harpooners.	Shots fired.	Whales caught.	Whales lost.
First	69	37	1
Second	53	26	2
Third	67	39	5
Fourth	51	23	5
Fifth	39	18	1
Sixth	52	31	4
Seventh	55	20	5
Eighth	2	1	0

July 4.—9 a.m., fog and rain, made the Whalesay Skerry Lighthouse ; 1 p.m. anchored in Bressay Sound, and landed our Shetland men ; 3 p.m. tripped our anchor and steamed for the Buchanness, which we made, and got safely into port the next day at 4 p.m.

Notes and harpooners' table from the log of the *Eclipse*, Captain David Gray, 1882. *Land and Water*, December 1882. *British Library*

THE WRECKING OF THE SS *MAZINTHIEN*, 1883

The *Mazinthien*, late of Peterhead and now stationed at Dundee, had been at sea only a few hours when she ran into a storm off Buchan Ness on 16 March 1883. The ship made at once for Peterhead Bay where her captain planned to weather the worst of it before continuing north to the fisheries.

Within hours the sea was raging and in spite of the crew's gallant attempt to secure her she began to drag anchor and drift towards the shore.

As great waves tore away her hatchways the crew's quarters flooded and much of her rigging broke away. By 2.30a.m. on the 17th she was in dire straits and it was then that the town's coastguard in charge, a Mr Goode, having spotted distress flares over the bay, alerted his team of volunteers.

Goode's men responded quickly and the horse drawn rescue apparatus wagon was soon on site. As the team struggled to get a line out to the ship they were drenched by the giant waves and had they not been secured by ropes many would have been washed away. A hawser was fired at the ship by rocket and, at the third attempt, found its target. On board ship, under the supervision of crewman John Hay, the men improvised a cradle using ropes blocks and planking. Hay was the first man to haul himself to shore along the hawser and by 11a.m. all twenty-eight of his mates were safely ashore.

Later in the day the storm subsided and boats were sent out to bring ashore the whale-boats and some of the crew's personal gear. The ship, having suffered a severe pounding, lay broken beyond repair.

LOST IN A GREENLAND FOG

Four whale boats from the Dundee ship *Chieftain* were bottlenosing north of Iceland on 26 May 1883, when a sudden dense fog fell around them. The grim events that followed were related by Thomas Southwell in the *Zoologist* two years later.

> The second mate's boat was picked up by the Norwegian schooner *Schrieder* and the crew transferred to their own vessel. The remaining three boats, in one of which there was a compass, determined to shape their course in company for Iceland, about two hundred miles distant; but on the 27th a severe gale commenced and the boats were separated; that commanded by the captain eventually reached Iceland all well, as did No.3, commanded by the spectioneer, one of the crew, however, dying shortly after he landed. The young lads in the fourth boat, in charge of Bain the harpooner, succumbed one after another, till Bain and steersman McIntosh were left alone. When after three days the storm abated McIntosh found Bain dead in the bow of the boat, and fearing he would not be able to restrain the pangs of hunger, the brave fellow to avoid temptation threw his dead comrade overboard, and after drifting about in a semi-conscious condition was, on the fourteenth day after leaving his ship, picked up by a shark-fishing vessel and conveyed to Iceland, the only survivor of the boat's crew; there both his legs had to be amputated.
>
> Thomas Southwell, *Zoologist*, 1885

'When after three days the storm abated McIntosh found Bain dead in the bow . . .'

David Gray, The Naturalist

I am proud of the friendship of a gentleman who has of late years done more than any other person to give the public information relative to the fauna of the far distant north.

This gentleman has spent twenty-two seasons at the North Pole, and each time has returned from his voyages he has brought us back some interesting news from his hunting grounds. I need hardly say that I refer to Capt. David Gray, of the steam whaling-ship *Eclipse*, of Peterhead, Aberdeenshire.

Frank Buckland, MA, HM Inspector of Fisheries.
'Notes and Jottings from Animal Life'

Buckland introduced himself to Captain Gray in the summer of 1870, while visiting Peterhead to inspect the Ugie salmon fishery on behalf of the Fisheries Board. He found Gray on board the *Eclipse* in the South Harbour. The ship had not long arrived from Greenland and her crew were busy scraping the last of her blubber cargo—the 'finks'—from the holding tanks. Buckland later recalled 'the whole ship smelt unpleasantly of oil, but the information Capt. Gray gave me was much too interesting for me to mind that.' The main topic of the day was the much vexed matter of a closed sealing time, a delay to the season in order that young seal cubs could develop to a stage where they might be able to fend for themselves. The annual slaughter of seals was prodigious. About 80,000 saddle-backs and a like number of hooded seals, were killed every season in the Greenland fishery, while the Newfoundland fishery destroyed an equal number. Gray and Buckland agreed that unless action was taken the race would soon become extinct.

Their campaign of mercy began on 22 July 1874 when Buckland addressed members of the Society for the Prevention of Cruelty to Animals at their Jubilee meeting. The situation was further explained in a letter to the *Times* the following March. Gray meanwhile prepared a case to present to Parliament—all too often he had witnessed the appalling sight of cubs left orphaned and helpless after the hunters had killed their mothers:

Fifteen or twenty years ago [wrote Captain Gray in 1876], a pack of seals would have extended in every direction as far as could be seen with a good telescope from the ship's mast head, the reflection darkening the sky above them. The case is greatly altered now: a pack very rarely exceeds a twentieth part of the above size, owing to the cruel manner in which they have been destroyed.

The motherless seals collect into lots of five or six and crawl about the ice, their heads fast becoming the biggest part of their bodies. Their cry is very like an infant's, and if one could imagine himself surrounded by four or five hundred thousand babies all crying at the pitch of their voices, he would have some idea of it. This is indeed a case where the Society for the Prevention of Cruelty to Animals would find full scope for carrying out its benevolent intentions, for there are no greater cruelties perpetrated on the face of the globe than at the Greenland seal fishing.

Captain David Gray, 'Habits of Arctic Seals' 1876

The evidence David Gray submitted to parliament was often shocking:

Three thousand is not an unusual number of seals to be slaughtered in a day by a single ship. At this work many of the men do not put themselves to the trouble of carrying clubs, but give the seal a tap on the nose with their foot to stun them, and skin them alive. They have often been seen to try to swim after having their skin taken off.

In 1876 an international close time was established prohibiting the killing of seals before 3 April, an arrangement which became effective the following year. 'I am quite certain', wrote Gray, 'that I could not have got the close time for seals without the aid of Frank Buckland. I first knew Mr Buckland in 1870; he was the man I wanted most to know in the world.'

Ship owners invested vast sums of money in their industry, paid their officers well and gave crews a good share of a season's profit. In return they demanded total dedication from all concerned. Commanders were expected to run an efficient ship, maintain law and order at sea and, of course, direct their skills and knowledge towards securing a profitable catch. In addition to their basic duties they were instructed to keep a close eye on the welfare and general behaviour of the whale and seal herds and submit detailed reports on their return to port.

David Gray pursued his zoological studies with great enthusiasm, and in time became a leading authority on such matters. He maintained a regular dialogue with Buckland, and his papers on the creatures' habits and environment were periodically featured in the natural history magazines of the day. Some brief descriptions and summaries of his texts were also used to accompany the works of Scottish wildlife artist Archibald Thorburn.

> Science is indebted to him for many facts elucidating the habits and structure of the Right Whale and the Hyperoodon [Bottlenose Whale], and humanity owes him a deep debt of gratitude for his successful efforts in establishing a close time for seals, by which he was mainly instrumental in abolishing, I trust for ever, the most cruel features of this occupation.
>
> Thomas Southwell on David Gray,
> *Zoologist*, March 1883

In the following passage, taken from a paper Gray prepared for the Natural History Society of Glasgow in 1882, the Captain reflects on the relationship between nursing Saddleback seals and their young.

> Towards night the old seals take to the water to feed, returning to their young in the morning, and lying on the ice with them the whole day. The young one draws upon its mother for nourishment at least once every hour, apparently to the old one's relief. When an old seal takes the ice she runs along until she catches the scent of her calf. When she comes to it there is a great display of kissing and other demonstrations of affection. When there are a number of young ones lying together some will draw in about to see if they can get a share of the attention. The old one immediately throws up her head and scolds very significantly, and if this does not drive them off she will use her teeth and claws very freely until she gets quietness. The young one will now poke its mother on the side with its nose until she turns over to it, when it immediately fixes on the teat; but if it has any difficulty in finding the place, the mother will direct it by scratching it back with her fin or hitching herself forward, and there the cub will remain for half an hour, the very picture of enjoyment. The supply seems to be so abundant that the milk can be seen flowing past the mouth of the young one. After it is satisfied it will roll about on its back, walloping its fins, or crawl away under the lee of its hummock [a mound of ice] to have a sleep. When an old one loses its young for a short time her state of distress is very

apparent; running over all the pieces round about, and screaming until she finds it. I have often watched the mother enticing her pup away from the neighbourhood of a ship. What patience she displays before she can get her young one to take the water, and then coaxed away little by little to what she considers a safe distance.

'Yesterday forenoon we were 240 miles from the nearest land, and two small birds from the linnet genus came fluttering up to the ship. How can they keep on the wing so long? – lat. obs., 67° 28.N; 0° 29.W. David Gray, log of the *Eclipse*, 19 March 1882.

To Captain Gray's generosity we are indebted for a valuable collection of Arctic animals, fish, and Esquimaux implements to be seen in the Arbuthnot Museum; and also for a splendid specimen of the Arctic bear, and the rare and valuable black eyebrowed albatross so much prized by naturalists. The last mentioned specimen, shot in lat.80°11N, long 4°E, has been greatly admired and frequently photographed by those interested in the study of natural history.

Peterhead Sentinel, 19 May 1896

June 15th: 80°N, 4°E. Shot an albatross—the only one, I suppose, ever seen here. Spread of wing 6ft. 10″, length 2ft., weight 8 lbs. Captain Gray, log of the *Eclipse*, 1878.

With his cruel bow he laid full low
The harmless Albatross.
The Rime of the Ancient Mariner, Samuel Taylor Coleridge.

Captain David Gray.
Peterhead.
23rd August 1885

W. H. Flower Esq.
Director of the Natural History Dept.
British Museum. N.H.
London S.W.

Dear Sir,
Your letter of 5th March reached here three days after I had sailed, and as I only returned last week you will see that it has been impossible for me to answer sooner.

It would be a very difficult and expensive operation to bring home a complete skeleton of a Greenland Whale. The whale-bone alone would cost at present £2,000 and where we get one whale there are usually more about and we are obliged to get rid of the Crang [carcass scrap] as soon as possible so as to be ready for more.

The only way I can think of is to employ one of the wintering ships at Cumberland Gulf to bring one, there they beach the Crangs for the use of the natives, and as they have a long winter to pass with nothing for the men to do, I should think there would be little difficulty in arranging to get one from them.

I do not hunt Bottle Nose whales now but I will undertake to get some of our Bottlenose fishers to bring home a series for you.

During my voyage I had a model of a full sized Greenland Whale made the dimension of which I took at the time the capture was made, its on an inch scale and I think I have made a very good job of it. I should like you to see it after I get it painted, I may have the pleasure of seeing you at the meeting of the British Association in Aberdeen when I can submit my model for your inspection.

I am dear Sir
Yours truly

David Gray

Gray's wooden model of a Greenland Right Whale (*Balaena mysticetus*) is still on exhibit in the museum. The register entry shows that the specimen from which the model was made was taken at lat.80°N on 17 June 1878 by the whale ship *Eclipse*. A similar model, again with a scale of 1 inch to the foot, was made by Captain Gray in 1885 and given to the Arbuthnot Museum in Peterhead. The latter is now on show in Aberdeen University's Department of Zoology.

The Captain continued his correspondence with the British Museum into his retiring years. Three letters, from Gray to Albert Gunther, Keeper of Zoology, remain on record in the museum archives. On 22 September 1893 he introduced his son Robert, and offered a collection of Arctic seabirds. The birds were sent a week later. His last communication was on 6 September 1894 when he sent a telegram reporting a beached rorqual near Peterhead.

'Molly'
(Fulmar)

'Burgomeister'
(Glaucous Gull)

'Rotchies'
(Little Auks)

ALEXANDER GRAY

Alexander was the last of the Gray brothers to take a ship's command. He served as chief officer aboard the *Eclipse* until 1870 when he accepted an invitation to accompany Prince Napoleon on an exploratory voyage to Spitzbergen. The Imperial Yacht, *Jerome Napoleon*, left Peterhead for Tromsø on 7 July, but on arrival at the Norwegian port grave news of the imminent Franco-Prussian war forced the Prince to abandon the expedition and return immediately to France. With his skills as an 'ice-pilot' no longer required Alec returned to Peterhead.

During the months that followed floods of emigrants left war-torn Europe for the United States; Robert Walker's diary records the fate of one of the less fortunate parties:

Nov 30th   A large Prussian Steamer with emigrants on Rattray, about 450 passengers and crew brought to Peterhead.

Dec 5th   The crew and passengers of the *Union* of Bremen are being taken on board a large steamer in the South Bay.

Dec 10th   Went to Rattray Head to see the wreck of the *Union* SS.

Alec Gray was given his first command in 1871. His ship, *Labrador*, was designed and built expressly for sealing and remained in his charge for nine prosperous seasons.

THE MARRIAGE OF CAPTAIN ALEC GRAY

The *Buchan Observer*, Friday 14 May 1880, announced the marriage of Alexander Gray to Euphemia Janet Comrie, of 21, Prince Street, Peterhead, daughter of Perth born surgeon Dr John Dickson Comrie and the late Euphemia T. Fettes. At the time Alec was living at 7, Castle Street, only a few doors from his birthplace.

ALICE GRAY LAUNCHES THE *EIRA*

Another Gray story appeared on the same page. The news of the day was the launch of the exploration vessel *Eira*, an auxilliary screw steam yacht built by Peterhead's Messrs. Stephen & Forbes for Mr Benjamin Leigh Smith, 'gentleman of London'. The ceremony of christening the vessel was 'gracefully performed' by Alice Gray, the ten year old daughter of Captain David Gray, now of Jamaica Street.

BROAD ST., PETERHEAD, LOOKING EAST. 9/1. G.W.W.

Peterhead Broadgate, c.1890. The three masts, standing clear against the harbour skyline, belong to a merchantman in the North Harbour's 'new' Graving Dock. The dry dock was built in the mid 1850s to cope with the whale fleet's demands, and was paid for by a local oil and bone levy.

The article went on, 'the day being fine a large number of people gathered around the quays to watch the progress of the launch, and some of the vessels in the harbour also displayed their colours'. As was the custom on such occasions the builders' apprentices were ducked in the wake of the new ship while others took a traditional thrashing from their masters. This was thought to bring luck to the ship and her makers, but on this occasion brought luck to neither. Trade was dismal for the ship builders of the north east and many workers soon found themselves jobless. Two years later the *Eira* was lost during her second visit to Franz Joseph Land and her crew were forced to endure the hazards of an Arctic winter on the frozen fields, surviving for much of the time on walrus meat.

The *Hope*, which had been forced home early that year with a damaged shaft, was duly commissioned by the Geographical Society to find the missing yacht and her crew, and with a government grant of £5,000 and a further £1,000 from the Society she left for the Barents Sea in June 1882.

Expedition leader Sir Allen William Young had prepared the ship for a long stay in Arctic waters but after only two months he and his crew – a combination of whalers and naval men – found Leigh Smith and his party at Matochkin Shar, on the west coast of Novya Zemlya.

'The Rescuers'. Expedition leader Sir Allen William Young (top hat) with the crew of the *Hope*, 1882.

The steam whaler *Erik*, late of Dundee, arrived at Peterhead for the first time under Captain Alec Gray on 30 January 1883. The docking of the 583 ton ship, the biggest whaler ever to be stationed at Peterhead, was by no means a simple task and did not pass without incident. Though Captain Birnie, the harbour master, warned the spectators away from the quayside, as the ship's ropes were thrown ashore three young lads were struck by a rope as it sprang tight. All three needed medical attention, but nobody was badly hurt.

Her first passage north was a stormy one with her bulwarks being carried away twice. Once at the ice the weather settled and after almost five months in Greenland waters the *Erik* brought home the produce of ninety-two bottlenose whales and 2,100 seals. Alec was the first of the three brothers home that year reporting that throughout the whole voyage he 'never saw nor spoke another vessel'.

SS *Hope* leaving the North Harbour, by ship's carpenter William Hutton. The tug on duty is probably *Pride o' Scotland*, resident in port throughout the 1880s.

'THE GREENLAND FLEET'

Preparations are to begin on Monday for rigging out and provisioning the vessels to start for Greenland. The *Hope* and *Erik* will leave about the usual time for the early sealing, and the *Eclipse*, as last season about the end of April for the old sealing and whaling. THE WAGES OF SEAMAN ARE SOMEWHAT LOWER THAN LAST SEASON. A.Bs are getting £2:5s. a month and ordinary seamen from 25s. to 35s. and 40s. in both cases the oil money being 1s. 3d. per ton for seal and 2s. for whale.

East Aberdeenshire Observer
Friday 11 February 1887

Whale alongside the *Eclipse*.

The ship and her master enjoyed five good seasons before her owners decided to close down business. Alec brought her home to Peterhead for the last time in 1887, sailing in the company of his brothers' *Hope* and *Eclipse*. Although David's ship made port that year with her smallest ever catch, she had still fared better than the others and was the only one of the little fleet—by now very much a family concern—to return a profit.

Log of the *Eclipse* 21 June 1887:

> 73°N, 16°W air 26°, sea 32°.
> Caught a whale, a female.
> 57ft. long, 12ft bone, yielding 27 tons of oil.
> The largest I have ever caught. (D.G.)

It was the 21st of June it being a glorious day,
The 'Clipse' she saw a whale fish,
And lowered all hands away.
The boats they pulled to leeward skipping o'er the sea,
And killed this noble whale fish,
Another Jubilee!

From the song *'Eclipse'*, 1887

The revelry that followed the great whale's capture was short lived. The *Eclipse* took nothing more in the Jubilee year and the Captains Gray returned to Peterhead in August with very little to celebrate. The *Erik* brought home only 9 tons and the *Hope* only 5 tons of seal oil.

The highlight of Alec Gray's season was the successful capture of 'a very fine live Polar bear for the Zoological Gardens in London'.

The jaw bones of the mighty bowhead were later donated to the South Kensington Museum.

Hope For Sale

In November 1887 both the *Erik* and the *Hope* were advertised for sale, the former at £5,000, the latter at £9,000. The lack of response to both offers reflected the state of business at the time; no offers were made for the *Erik* at her sale in the Royal Oak Hotel, and the *Hope* remained under John Gray at Peterhead until 1891 when she was transferred to Newfoundland for £1,000 less than the asking price.

The *Windward* was Alec Gray's third and final Peterhead command, his alliance with her lasting only three years. Realising the futility of the depleted fleet's efforts, he left Peterhead in 1890 for a new career, rejoining his old ship the *Erik*, by now a supply ship for the Hudson's Bay Company's outposts.

> In his earlier years Captain Alexander Gray prosecuted whale and seal fishing like his brothers, and returned with numerous successful catches, but in later years he entered the service of the Hudson's Bay Co. and for a period of over thirty years was engaged in voyaging between London and Hudson Bay, in the *Erik*, the *Pelican*, and other vessels, bringing home the produce collected at the Company's stations in the Hudson Bay region.
> *Buchan Observer*, Tuesday 13 December 1910

Alec, Euphemia, and their daughters made their new home at 'Benhilton', Sutton, to the south of London's dockland. It was at nearby Farleigh that the retired captain died on 3 December 1910. He was 75 years old.

SS *Erik* continued to supply the settlements of Canada's north west coast until her fatal encounter with a U-Boat during World War I.

BALEINIER A VAPEUR HOPE D'ABERDEEN 1887
Den de M. Christen, ingénieur

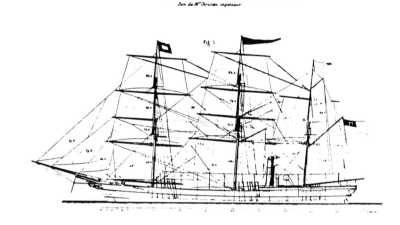

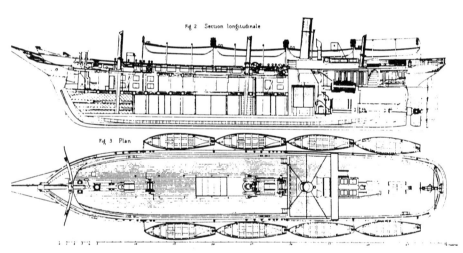

When the *Hope* came up for sale in 1887 an additional set of plans and information was drawn up for the French Canadian market.

'The Links', Peterhead (1880-1991).
Built for Captain David Gray in 1880, 'The Links' remained the Gray's family home until May 1919 when the house was sold to local fish curer John Sutherland.

For many years the jaw bone of a whale, harpooned by Robert Gray in July 1884, stood in the grounds, eventually finding a use as a children's garden swing.

The Old House Becomes a Hospital.
In 1930 the John Davidson Buchan Fund, with a donation of £1,000, was established to raise money to build a new town hospital. A further £5,000 was donated four years later by Mr W B Shewan of Eastburn and with the help of further donations, large and small, the Town Council bought 'The Links' from the Sutherlands in October 1938 and began conversion work.

THE HARBOUR OF REFUGE

For a number of years Captain David Gray was a member of the harbour board, and for a short period was also in the Town Council. But if he cared little for the honour of public office, he did much to encourage and develop local enterprise. In the enquiry held by Sir George Nares as to the most suitable place for a harbour of refuge on the east coast of Scotland, Captain Gray gave important and convincing evidence in favour of Peterhead.

Peterhead Sentinel & Buchan Journal, 1896

Though the notion of an east coast harbour of refuge had been under discussion since the early 1840s it was not until 1881 that Gladstone's government established a committee of enquiry into the project. The cities and towns of the coast were then invited to put forward their individual cases, and with so much at stake the competition was strong and the battle hard fought. In September 1883 the commission, headed by The Hon. Mr Chamberlain, President of the Board of Trade, arrived at Peterhead on board the SS *Galatea* to hear the local delegates points of view and inspect the town's plans. Before the commissioners left for Aberdeen and Granton they were entertained aboard the *Eclipse* and given, by way of entertainment, a demonstration of 'the mode of firing the harpoon gun and the hand held harpoon'. They were also allowed to inspect the cargo of bottlenose oil.

The town had a lot in its favour. The position was ideal, and the bay, with Keith Inch to the north and Salthouse Head to the south, already formed a haven of sorts. For raw materials the commission would not have to look further than nearby Stirling Hill where a vast amount of granite lay untapped.

After much discussion and heated debate Peterhead won the day, and an Act of Parliament, passed in 1886, authorised planners and builders to proceed with their work.

HARD LABOUR

The problem of labour was overcome by the building of a Convict Prison to the south of the bay. The first of the convicts arrived in 1888, and after completing work on the prison began the construction of the giant breakwaters that would in time become the town's best known landmarks.

The piers were constructed from concrete blocks, each weighing between thirty and fifty tons, faced with granite and placed on a rough stone foundation. Armed guards watched over convict gangs as they blasted granite from the quarry at Stirling Hill and sent it down to the shore by way of a purpose built railway. At Salt Head, secure inside the walls of the Admiralty Yard, the train was unloaded and under the supervision of local masons another team of convicts prepared the giant blocks.

Work on the project went on for many years and the booming sound of 'blasting', like distant artillery, at Stirling Hill was a part of Peterhead's daily routine for more than fifty years.

THE ANTARCTIC EXPERIMENT

The feasibility of Scottish vessels hunting the antarctic seas was the subject of a detailed investigation by David and John Gray. Though their report, first published in 1877 and reviewed in 1891, was well received by their peers both at home and abroad, the great plan came to nothing. (It may well be that Gray had upgraded his ship's steam-power back in 1876 in order that the *Eclipse* might one day lead the way south).

With the brothers' advice and financial support Dundee's Tay Whaling Company sent four ships to the southern waters in September 1892. David Gray's old ship the *Active* and another Peterhead vessel, *Polar Star*, now fitted for steam and stationed at Dundee, made their way south with the auxilliary steamers *Balaena* and *Diana*. Though they fared quite well their catch did not justify any further investment, and the fate of the Gray whalers was sealed.

The End of an Era

Captain John Gray Jnr died at Clifton House on 2 May 1892. His sons left Peterhead, Edward Seymour to the Transvaal, John Hope to Rhodesia, and Alexander Geary to Natal. Later that same year the *Eclipse* was sold to Dundee, but not without protest, her final exit from Peterhead—on Saturday 4 February 1893—being every bit as dramatic as her eclipsed debut at Aberdeen twenty-five years earlier.

> The *Eclipse* was very unwilling to go. The order was given to leave Peterhead, but, like an infuriated animal that is being forced against its will, the steamer in her exit from the harbour ran into and damaged at least two ships and several fishing boats, and on Friday afternoon stuck fast in mid-channel, remaining there till the tide next day.
>
> *Aberdeen Free Press*, February 1893

SS *Windward* – last of the Peterhead whalers – in the North Harbour.

SS *Eclipse* continued whaling from Dundee until 1909 when she was sold to Norway. Peterhead's most celebrated ship ended her career as a research vessel under the Russian flag, based in the White Sea. Renamed *Lomonosov* she made routine voyages between Archangel and Murmansk until the 1930s, maybe even later. Her name was removed from the Lloyds Register in 1961.

THE LAST VOYAGE OF DAVID GRAY

On Tuesday 18 April 1893 David Gray took the *Windward* out of Peterhead for the last time. Her only kill, on 6 May at 78°N, was the last by a Peterhead ship and marked the end of her home port's hundred year war on the northern herds.

Captain Gray, having suffered gout for several years, became seriously ill during the voyage and as *Windward* was tied up, on 7 August 1893, Peterhead's greatest shipmaster said farewell to the sea.

> The retirement of Captain David Gray marks the closing epoch in the history of the Peterhead fishery, and for the first time since 1811 the arctic seas of either Greenland or Davis Straits have remained unvisited by one or more of his family, and with the last Gray I fear this once thriving industry, which his family has done so much to promote, so far as his native port of Peterhead is concerned, has virtually come to an end.
>
> Thomas Southwell, *Zoologist* 1893

For a man whose life had been so rich in adventure retirement brought few pleasures. From his study, on the first floor of the Links, Gray watched with great interest as ships and fishing boats made their way in and out of the South Harbour. The gigantic south breakwater was by now slowly making its way across Peterhead Bay, a sight that must have given the commander satisfaction—the great Harbour of Refuge that he and his associates had fought so long and hard for was at last becoming a reality. The future of his home town was secure!

Captain Gray suffered his painful illness with characteristic bravery until, in early May 1896, he was struck down by a severe apoplectic shock from which he was not to recover.

David Gray died at the Links on the evening of 16 May 1896. He was buried at the Peterhead Cemetery, Constitution Street, four days later.

> No name is more closely associated with the commercial prosperity of our good town than that of Captain David Gray. His memory will long

be cherished as one of Peterhead's most distinguished townsmen—a man of the highest character, widely respected, and deservedly honoured both at home and abroad.

Peterhead Sentinel, May 1896

AFTER THE STORM

Peterhead maintained its interest in whaling and sealing until the 1920s through the annual voyages of the ketch *Albert* to and from Black Lead Island in the Cumberland Gulf (lat.64°58′N, long.66°13′W).

Towards the end of the Peterhead whaling era it became the custom for a few crewmen from each ship to winter with the 'Yaks' (Eskimos), hunting bears, walrus and narwhals until their ship returned in the spring to collect the spoils. Fred Cameron, of the *Albert* spent the years 1914–18 at Peterhead's Black Lead settlement and knew nothing of the Great War until he was relieved in 1919!

In 1894 the voyage of the *Eclipse* from Dundee to Davis Straits was logged by a Seaman Redgrave.

October 10th, Cumberland Gulf:
We were at once boarded by a cargo of Female Yaks called Koonies and every man had his squaw. It was positively sickening. If people call that whaling the sooner it is stopped the better!

November:
After a voyage of Headwinds and Storms and losing a poor fellow overboard, another case of inhumanity as the ship continued to her course—but sailors are only dogs after all—we got back on the 21st. I think I have said nearly all, but if there is anything let me know, and I hope it will fill up a dull New-Years evening.

Redgraves Log, 1894

'A home on the frozen deep'
Captain's Cabin, SS *Eclipse*, 1888.

David Gray and Bob, 1888.

THE GRAYS OF PETERHEAD

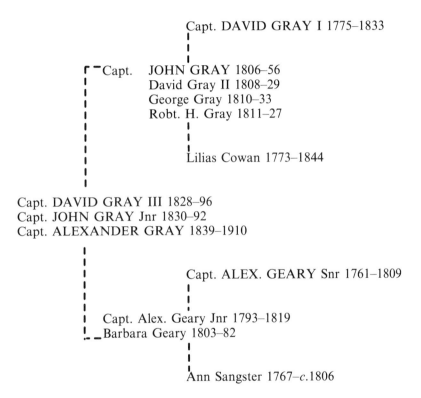

Capt. DAVID GRAY I 1775–1833

Capt. JOHN GRAY 1806–56
David Gray II 1808–29
George Gray 1810–33
Robt. H. Gray 1811–27

Lilias Cowan 1773–1844

Capt. DAVID GRAY III 1828–96
Capt. JOHN GRAY Jnr 1830–92
Capt. ALEXANDER GRAY 1839–1910

Capt. ALEX. GEARY Snr 1761–1809

Capt. Alex. Geary Jnr 1793–1819
Barbara Geary 1803–82

Ann Sangster 1767–c.1806

For the sake of brevity only those family members directly involved in the whale fishing have been listed above. Though all four of David Gray I's sons joined the merchant service as young apprentice sailors only John, the eldest, made the rank of Captain. Robert Gray, who at one time had served as a line manager aboard the whaler *Dexterity*, was drowned while whaling at Davis Straits in the spring of 1827. David Gray II was twenty-one years old when he suffered the same fate, again at Davis Straits, two years later. George died as his ship lay in Hamburg docks in May 1833, the cause of his death unknown.

THE COMMANDERS AND THEIR COMMANDS

Alexander Geary:
Robert 1798–1801
Hope 1803–09

Alexander Geary Jnr:
Enterprise 1814–15
Dexterity 1816–19

David Gray I:
Perseverance 1811–12
Active 1813–25
Perseverance 1826

John Gray Snr:
Active 1826–27
Alpheus 1828
Based at Kirkcaldy, 1829–35
Eclipse 1836–56

David Gray III:
North of Scotland 1849–52
Active (2) 1853–66
Eclipse SS 1867–91
Windward SS 1893

John Gray Jnr:
Queen 1852–61
Mazinthien 1862–72
Hope SS 1873–91

Alexander Gray:
Labrador 1871–79
Erik SS 1883–87
Windward SS 1888–91

The family of Captain David Gray III and Amelia Walker, 1888.
Robert, William, Alice, Lily, Vitie.
Peggie, Jimmy, Francis, David, Doris, Jean.

THE GRAY'S FAMILY FILE

Abbreviations used in Family File
bapt. baptised; b. born; bur. buried; cert. certified; *c. circa*, dau. daughter; d. died; m. married; MO Medical Officer; MD Doctor of Medicine; P.D. Peterhead; w. witnessed Ind. Independent; i. interred.

Alexander Geary 1761–1809, Ann Sangster 1767–c.1806. m. P.D. *c*.1790.

Alexander Geary, Ship's Master, buried P.D. 19 Dec, 1809, age 48. St Peter's Old Kirk-yard.

Ann Sangster bapt. 7 Sept 1767, P.D. dau. of John Sangster in Ronheads. Witnessed by John and Alex Gray. (She was buried in P.D. Old Kirkyard 19 Nov 1800. The year seems to have been wrongly recorded as she had two children after that date.)

FAMILY:

JEAN bapt. 14 Nov 1791.

ALEXANDER bapt. 1 Oct 1793. m. Jessie Alexander, of Cruden, 13 Dec 1814, P.D. Ship's Master, died 1819. Buried 4 Aug P.D. Old Kirkyard.

MARY bapt. 12 Oct 1795. m. Charles McKenzie 9 Jan 1820, P.D. Buried 5 Nov 1841, aged 45 yrs.

ELIZABETH bapt. 12 Sept 1779. m John Scott (1797–1834).

(The above all w. by John Sangster and John Ogston)

JANET bapt. 2 July 1799. m. Charles Tod 13 Jan 1825. i. 11 May 1888, 'Jessie' Tod, age 88, St Peter Street.

KATHERINE bapt. 3 July 1801. m. Capt. Wm. Ogston, P.D. i. 18 Feb 1901, Catherine G. Ogston, age 99, Prince Street. (Wm. Ogston bapt. 11 March 1799, P.D. son of Robert Ogston. Buried 1 May 1837, Old Kirkyard).

BARBARA (1803–82). bapt. w. by Robt. Geary and James Sangster, 1 May 1803.

ANN bapt. 17 Oct 1805.

David Gray I 1775–1833, Lilias Cowan 1773–1844. (Came to P.D. from South Shields 1810)

David Gray of Keith Inch d. 1 July, bur. 20 July 1833 P.D. Old Kirkyard, age 57, Ship's Master. (Drowned while fishing in South Bay)

'Lily' Cowan of Keith Inch d. 16 Jan, bur. 20 Jan 1844 P.D. Old Kirkyard, age 71. (Died in a fire at her home in Castle Street)

FAMILY:

MARGARET 1802- bapt. 3 Jan 1802, South Shields.

JOHN (1806–56) bapt. 2 Feb 1806, South Shields.

DAVID (1808–29) bapt. 14 Feb 1808, South Shields. d. Davis Strait, bur. 1829 P.D. Old Kirkyard.

GEORGE ARBUTHNOT bapt. 27 Dec 1810 w. by Capt. John Souter and Capt. Thomas Philips. d. 1833 bur. 22 May 1833, age 23.

ROBERT HUTCHISON b. 1811, P.D., bapt. 24 May 1813, d. 1827, Davis Strait, bur. 3 June 1827, aged 17.

ELIZA (1816–1825) bur. Eliza Gray of Keith Inch, 9 Oct 1825, age 9.

David (II) and Robert both drowned at Davis Straits. George—the first of the line to be born in Peterhead for at least two generations—died in Hamburg in 1833.

NB: Also buried in the Gray's family plot at P.D.'s Old Kirkyard is a 13 year old 'Esquimaux' boy, Jacob Johannes. He was buried there on 21 May 1826. An Eskimo woman named Mary was buried at the same time in a grave nearby (see p. 17)

John Gray 1806–56, Barbara Geary 1803–82.
m. 18 Dec 1827, P.D.

John Gray b. Feb 1806, South Shields. Died on board his ship *Eclipse* at Davis Strait, 11 Aug 1856 (9.30a.m.). Cardiac Dropsy, certified by Elias Johnston, M.O. on board. Signed by Chief Officer George Murray. bur. at P.D. Old Kirkyard 15 Sept 1856.

Barbara Geary bapt. 1 May 1803. d. 14 June 1882, aged 79, 11 Castle Street, P.D. (12 noon); dau. of Alex Geary, Shipmaster, and Ann Geary m.s. Sangster; cert. by Stephen M.D. Signed John Gray, son, present.

FAMILY:
DAVID, III 1828–96.
JOHN. 1830–92.
ANN. b. 1832, Kirkcaldy, Fifeshire.
ELIZA. bapt. 12 Oct 1835. m. Peter Christie.
GEORGINA. bapt. 29 Oct 1837. m. William Gray.
ALEXANDER. 1839–1910.

P.D. Census 1841: John Gray, listed as living at Castle Street in seaman's listing.

Pool Lane (off Castle Street)

Barbara Gray,	35yrs.	shipmaster's wife.
David	12yrs.	son.
John	10yrs.	son.
Ann	9yrs.	dau.
Eliza	5yrs.	dau.
Georgina	3yrs.	dau.
Alexander	2yrs.	son.
Agnes Liddle	20yrs.	servant.
Ann Cowans	30yrs.	shipmaster's wife.
Ann	1yr.	dau.
David	4mths.	son.

Also at Pool Lane—Lillie Gray, 65, Ind. and David 12. [David listed with his mother AND his grandmother]

P.D. Census 1851, Castle St. Keith Inch:
(Sch. 40.)

Barbara Gray,	shipmaster's wife,	45yrs.	born P.D.
Ann	dau.	19yrs.	born Kirkcaldy.
Eliza	dau.	14yrs.	born P.D.
Georgina	dau.	13yrs.	born P.D.
Alexander	son.	12yrs.	born P.D.

David Gray III 1828–96, Isabella Gamack Law 1829–58.
m. 11 Dec 1851, P.D.

David Gray bapt. 26 Oct 1828, son of John Gray, Shipmaster, Peterhead, w. by David Gray I and Capt. John Birny; d. at his home 'The Links', P.D. 16 May 1896 (6p.m.), aged 67, after 10 years of gout. Signed Alexander Gray (brother) of 45 King Street P.D. bur. the Cemetery, Landale Street.

Isabella Gamack Law b. 1829, dau. of George Law, merchant, and Isabella Milne. She died soon after the birth of her fourth child (David) of Erysiphilas (an infection contracted during the birth see p.000) on 28 Sept 1858 at 14 Harbour Street P.D. Cert. by Anderson, surgeon. Signed David Gray, husband present. bur. 2 Oct P.D. Old Kirkyard.

FAMILY:

ISABELLA b. 15 Aug 1853, 14 Harbour Street. d. 29 March 1914, (m. James Bruce, Cooper, 1854–1916, of Prince St). bur. 1 April P.D. Old Kirkyard.

BARBARA GEARIE b. 17 June 1855 (3p.m.) 14 Harbour Street (m. Richard Badenach Crabb 28 Nov 1881; three daughters).

JOHN b. 5 Sept 1856, Harbour Street. d. 16 Sept 1879. Merchant Seaman.

DAVID b. 7 Sept 1858 (9.30a.m.) Harbour Street. Signed David Gray, father present. d. 20 Sept 1858. (9a.m.) Erysiphilas, cert. by Anderson, Surgeon, signed D. Gray, father, present (14 days old).

P.D. Census 1841, Broad Street (north):

George Law,	45yrs.	Grocer.
Isabella,	40yrs.	
John,	13yrs.	
ISABELLA,	11yrs.	
George,	9yrs.	

P.D. Census 1861, 14 Harbour Street

Georgina,	23 yrs.	(D.G.'s sister) Unmarried, Housekeeper
Isabella	7 yrs.	dau (of D.G.) Scholar.
Barbara G.	5 yrs.	"
John,	4 yrs.	son.

(All the above born Peterhead).
Christian Lawrance, 24 yrs.   Unmarried, Servant born P.D.

NB: Captain Gray employed his sister, Georgina, as his housekeeper after the death of his wife, Isabella Law.

David Gray III 1828–96, Amelia Walker 1841–1937.
m. 11 Nov 1863, P.D.

Amelia Walker (D.G.'s second wife) was born in 1841 the daughter of Robert

Walker (landowner, P.D. 1816–90) of Richmond, P.D. and Violet Sutter (1815–1902, dau. of Capt. John Sutter and Isabella Ogilvie.) Amelia d. 31 Dec 1937, age 96, at The Elms, Bieldside, East Peterculter, by Aberdeen. Signed by James Gray (son) of The Croft, Game Keepers Road, Barnton, Midlothian. bur. 3 Jan 1938 at Constitution Cemetery, P.D.

FAMILY:
Born at 14 Harbour Street:
ROBERT WALKER b. 8 Oct 1864 (7a.m.). Served as chief officer on his father's ship *Eclipse* 1883–90, leaving the sea to become a doctor (Aberdeen Medical School) sometime in Tezpur, Assam, and Bonny, Nigerian coast, then Bushey Herts and Devon.
WILLIAM LUMSDEN b. 8 Oct 1864 (7.30a.m.) Signed David Gray, father, not present. (Unmarried tea planter in Assam, died abroad c.1910.)

Born at 8 Jamaica Street:
MARGARET b. 7 May 1866. d. 25 Sept 1866 at Richmond P.D. Signed Robert Walker, grandfather.
MAGNUS b. 13 Nov 1867. d. 12 Jan 1887, USA.
VIOLET b. 13 Aug 1869. d. 11 Sept 1869.
ALICE b. 20 Oct 1870.
LILIAS 'Lily' b. 11 July, 1872. (m. Arthur Bristow (1868–1917), engineer, Bury St Edmunds: 2 sons).
VIOLET 'Vitie' b. 19 June 1874. (m. Andrew J. Volum 28 Dec 1911) d. c.1960.
JANE b. 10 July 1876. Signed Jane Walker, aunt (m. Stanley Thorburn, banker, 1920, Colombo. Retired to St Albans, d. 1962).

Born at 15 Jamaica Street:
DORIS b. May 20 1878. Signed Barbara G. Gray, sister (m. Frederick Wernham. Two sons. d. 1971).
DAVID b. 21 July 1879. Signed Annie Walker, aunt. (m. Janet Rennie 1910). d. 1954, USA.
FRANCIS AMELIA b. 17 Dec 1880. Signed by aunt Violet Walker of Richmond.

Born at 'The Links':
JAMES b. 1 Aug 1882. Signed Robt. W. Gray, brother. Harbour Master, Colombo, Sri Lanka (Ceylon). (m. Ada Ritson 1912). Retired to Edinburgh – engineer/craftsman. d. 1953.
MARGARET, 'Peggie', b. 27 May 1884; d. 22 April 1889.

P.D. Census 1871, 8 Jamaica Street

Amelia Gray,	29 yrs.	Shipmaster's wife.	Born Peterhead.
Barbara	15 yrs.	dau. (step)	,, ,,
John	14 yrs.	son (step)	,, ,,
Robert	6 yrs.	son scholar	,, ,,
William	6 yrs.	,, ,,	,, ,,

Magnus	3 yrs.	"	"	"
Alice	5 mths.	dau.	"	"
Hellen Philips,	25 yrs.	servant.	Born Cruden.	
Isobella Lawrance,	21 yrs.	"	"	Peterhead.
Jane Taylor,	25 yrs.	"	"	New Deer.

P.D. Census 1881.
13–15 Jamaica Street.

David Gray	52 yrs.	Master of a Whaler.	Born P.D.
Amelia	39 yrs.	wife.	
Barbara G.	25 yrs.	dau. unmarried.	
William	16 yrs.	son scholar	
Alice	10 yrs.	dau. "	
Lilias	8 yrs.		
Violet	6 yrs.		
Jean (Jane)	4 yrs.		
Doris	2 yrs.		
David	1 yr.		
Francis	3 mths.		

P.D. Census 1891.
'The Links'

David Gray	62 yrs.	Shipmaster	Born P.D.
Amelia	49 yrs.	wife	"
Robert W.	26 yrs.	student (medical)	"
Alice	20 yrs.	"	"
Lilias	18 yrs.	"	"
Violet	16 yrs.	"	"
Jane	14 yrs.	"	"
Doris	12 yrs.	"	"
David	11 yrs.	"	"
Frances (dau.)	10 yrs.	"	"
James	8 yrs.	"	"
Ann Stephen	24 yrs.	cook, dom. serv.	"
Margaret Summers	27 yrs.	house maid	"

John Gray Jnr 1830–92, Emily Lindsay 1841–1926.
m. 20 Dec 1866, Marykirk, Kincardine.

John Gray Jnr bapt. 18 Sept 1830, w. by David Gray I and Capt. John Birny.
d. 2 May 1892 (2a.m.) 'Clifton House', Queen St. P.D. age 61. Signed
David Gray (brother) 'The Links' P.D.
Emily Lindsay b. Montrose, 1841. d. 4 Nov 1926 in P.D. age 85.

FAMILY:
Born at 14 Harbour Street:
EMILY LINDSAY b. 28 June 1868.
EDITH b. 3 May 1870. Signed by David Gray, uncle.

Born at 22 Jamaica Street:
ANNIE LOUISA b. 11 May 1872. Signed Edith Lindsay.
EDWARD SEYMOUR b. 9 July 1873. d. 13 Oct 1925, Transvaal, age 52.
HELLEN ELLIOT b. 23 June 1875.
JOHN HOPE b. 15 May 1877, P.D. d. 24 Dec 1911, Rhodesia, aged 34.
ALEXANDER GEARY b. 17 June 1879, 20 Jamaica Street. d. 29 May 1916,
    Natal, age 36.

Born at 'Clifton House' 96 Queen Street.
IDA ROSE b. 30 June 1882, P.D. d. 11 Dec 1884.

P.D. Census 1871, 14 Harbour Street.
(previously owned by his brother David)

Emily Gray	31 yrs.	Shipmaster's wife.	Born Montrose.
Emily	2 yrs.	dau.	Born Peterhead.
Edith	11 mths.	"	" "
Margaret Forbes	20 yrs.	servant.	" "
Christian Clubb	18 yrs.	"	" "

P.D. Census 1881.

'Clifton House', 96 Queen Street.

John Gray	50 yrs.	Shipmaster at Greenland fishery.	
Emily	41 yrs.	wife.	Born Montrose
Emily	12 yrs.	dau. scholar.	Born P.D.
Edith	10 yrs.	dau.	" "
Annie Lousa	8 yrs.	dau.	" "
Edward Seymour	7 yrs.	son.	" "
Hellen Elliot	5 yrs.	dau.	" "
John Hope	3 yrs.	son.	"
Alexander Geary	1 yr.	son.	"
Annie Eliza Pattula?	19 yrs,	niece, unmarried, student.	
Margaret Wallace	24 yrs.	servant, unmarried.	Born P.D.
Jemima E. Hill	16 yrs.	"	" "

P.D. Census 1891.
96, Queen St.
(John Gray absent)

Emily Gray	51 yrs.		Born Montrose
Annie L.	18 yrs.		Born P.D.
Edward S.	17 yrs.	sailor	"

Helen E.	15 yrs.	scholar	,,
John H.	13 yrs.	,,	,,
Alex G.	11 yrs.	,,	,,
Barbara Shand	17 yrs.	gen. serv.	,,

Alexander Gray 1839–1910, Euphemia J. Comrie 1856- m. 13 May 1880, 21 Prince Street, P.D. (Rev James Stewart)

Alex Gray b. Castle Street, Keith Inch, bapt. 12 June 1839, w. by Alex Mitchell, ship owner, and Charles Todd, Collector of Shore Dues. d. 3 Dec 1910, Benhilton, Farleigh, Sutton, Surry. (At the time of his marriage living at 7 Castle Street, Keith Inch).

Euphemia Janet Comrie b. P.D. 1856, dau. of Dr John Dickson Comrie (b. 1822 Perth) and Euphemia Torrence Fettes. (Dr Comrie later married for a second time to Helen K. m.s. unknown, born New York, USA 1839).

FAMILY:
Born at 45 King Street:
ETHEL BARBARA b. 17 June 1882.
DOROTHY b. 14 Oct 1883.
EUPHEMIA b. 19 Aug 1885.
COLIN JOHN b. 4 Nov 1886.
WILLIAM b. 26 July 1888. Signed John Gray, uncle. d. 4 Aug 1888. bur. P.D. Cemetery.

P.D. Census 1891.
45 King St.

Alexander Gray,	51 yrs.	Shipmaster	Born P.D.
Euphemia J.	40 yrs.		,,
Ethel Barbara	8 yrs.		,,
Dorothy	7 yrs.		,,
Euphemia	5 yrs.		,,
Colin	4 yrs.		,,
Helen D. Knights	17 yrs.	governess	Born Norwich.
Harriet Smith	23 yrs.	cook, serv.	Born P.D.
Elsie Smith	25 yrs.	dom. serv.	Born Crimond.

BIBLIOGRAPHY

Arbuthnot, John George, Journal of a Voyage to the Greenland Seal and Whale Fishing, the *Eclipse*, 1852 (North East Libraries, Oldmeldrum).

—— Journal of the Whale Ship *Active*, 1853 (North East Libraries, Oldmeldrum).

Bompas, George C, *Life of Frank Buckland* (Smith, Elder & Co., 1885).

Bonner-Smith, D, 'The Mutiny at the Nore, 1797', *Mariner's Mirror*, Vol 33, 1947.

Buchan, Alex, *The Port of Peterhead* (P Scrogie Ltd).

Buchan, Peter, *Fit Like Skipper?* (*Aberdeen Journals*, 1985).

Buckland, Francis Trevelyan, Log-book of a Fisherman & Zoologist (Chapman & Hall, 1876).

—— Notes and Jottings from Animal Life (Smith, Elder & Co., 1887).

Cook, John, Pursuing the Whale (John Murray, 1926).

Dugan, James, The Great Mutiny (Andre Deutsch, 1966).

Edwards, Owen D, Quest for Sherlock Holmes (Mainstream Publications, 1983).

Egede, Hans, Description of Greenland (W H Reid; and Baldwin, Cradock & Joy, 1818).

Findlay, James Thomas, A History of Peterhead (P Scrogie Ltd, 1933).

Gray, David, Habits of Whales, *Land and Water*, 1878.

—— After the Whales and Young Seals, *Land and Water*, December 1882 (British Newspaper Library).

Gray, James, 'The Peterhead Whaling Ship *Eclipse*', *Mariner's Mirror*, Vol 23, 1937.

Gray, Dr Robert Walker, 'Peterhead Sealers and Whalers', *The Scottish Naturalist*, 1932, 1933.

—— 'Peterhead & the Greenland Sea', *Transactions of the Buchan Field Club*, Vol 16, 1939-42.

Harmer, Sir Sidney, 'The History of Whaling', *Proceedings of the Linnean Society*, 1927.

Henderson, David S, *Fishing for the Whale* (Dundee, 1972).

Jackson, Rear Admiral T S, *Logs of Great Sea Fights*, Vol 1 (Navy Records Society, 1899).

Jones, A G E, 'Captain Robert Martin, a Peterhead Whaling Master in the 19th Century', *Scottish Geographical Magazine*, Vol 85, 1969.

Laing, Dr, 'Peterhead and its Mineral Wells', 1792.

Lawrie, Alistair, H Matthews and D Ritchie, *Glimmer of Cold Brine* (Aberdeen University Press, 1988).

Leslie, Sir John, *Discovery and Adventure in the Polar Seas and Regions* (T Nelson & Sons, 1852).

Lloyd, C and J Coulter, *Medicine and the Navy*, Vol 3 (E & S Livingstone Ltd, 1961).

Lubbock, Basil, *The Arctic Whalers* (Brown, Ferguson & Son Ltd, 1937)

MacLeod, Innes (ed) *To the Greenland Whaling*, Alex Trotter's, Journal of the voyage of the *Enterprise*, 1856 (The Thule Press, Sandwick, 1979)

Milne, Dr Alexander, 'Peterhead and the Arctic Whale Fishery', in Tocher's *The Book of Buchan*, Jubilee Volume (Aberdeen, 1943).

Neish, Robert, *Old Peterhead* (P Scrogie Ltd, 1950).

Pratt, Rev John B, *Buchan* (Aberdeen, 1858).

Savours, Anne (ed) Journal of a Whaling Voyage from Dundee to Davis Straits. *Polar Record*, Vol 10, 1960.

Scoresby, William Jnr, *An Account of the Arctic Regions*, Vols 1 and 2 (Edinburgh, 1820).

—— *Journal of a Voyage to the Northern Whale-Fishery* (Edinburgh, 1823).

Shewan, Captain Andrew, The Great Days of Sail (Conway Maritime Press, Greenwich)

Shuldham-Shaw, Patrick and Emily B Lyle (eds) The Greig-Duncan Folk Song Collection, Vol 1 (Aberdeen University Press, 1990).

Southwell, Thomas, 'Notes on the Seal and Whale Fishery', The Zoologist, February 1882- April 1893.

Spence, Bill, Harpooned (Conway Maritime Press, 1980).

Thomson, J Inches, 'Voyages and Wanderings in Far-off Seas and Lands'.

Tocher, J F (ed) The Book of Buchan (Peterhead, 1910).

Publications consulted: *Buchan Observer, Peterhead Sentinel & Buchan Journal, Banffshire Journal, Aberdeen Daily Free Press, Aberdeen Free Press and Buchan News, Aberdeen Herald, Aberdeen Chronicle, East Aberdeenshire Observer, Peterhead Kalendar*, 1853; *Peterhead Almanac and Directory*, 1864; *Directory of Scotland*, Pigot and Co., 1837.

Family Research sources: Registration of Births Deaths and Marriages: Aberdeen, Peterhead and Montrose. Old Parish Records: Peterhead and Kirkcaldy. Census Records: Peterhead. Interment Records: Peterhead.

Additional sources of information: The Private Diaries of Robert Walker of Richmond (courtesy of Frederick Gray Wernham, Elgin); Royal National Lifeboat Institution, Archive Records (Barry Cox, Hon Librarian, Poole, Dorset); Natural History Museum, London (John C Thackray, Archivist, British Museum); Captain David Gray's Papers, Grampian Regional Archives, Old Aberdeen House; Public Records Office, Kew; Scottish Records Office, Edinburgh; Grampian Health Board Archives (Fiona Watson); Sederunt Records of Peterhead Harbour Trustees (1806-1948); Arbuthnot Museum, Peterhead; The Royal Museums, Edinburgh; Dundee Museum, Dundee.